HOW TO VOTE!

OR, THE REPERCUSSIONS OF POLITICAL AMBITION AND PERSONAL RIVALRIES WITHIN STUDENT LEADERSHIP AND MEDIA ORGANISATIONS IN THE CONTEXT OF THE POST-COVID-19 NEOLIBERAL UNIVERSITY INSTITUTION

JULIAN LARNACH

CURRENCY PRESS
The performing arts publisher

CURRENT THEATRE SERIES

First published in 2022
by Currency Press Pty Ltd,
PO Box 2287, Strawberry Hills, NSW, 2012, Australia
enquiries@currency.com.au
www.currency.com.au

in association with Canberra Youth Theatre

Copyright: *How to Vote* © Julian Larnach, 2022.

COPYING FOR EDUCATIONAL PURPOSES

The Australian *Copyright Act 1968* [Act] allows a maximum of one chapter or 10% of this book, whichever is the greater, to be copied by any educational institution for its educational purposes provided that that educational institution [or the body that administers it] has given a remuneration notice to Copyright Agency [CA] under the Act.
For details of the CA licence for educational institutions contact CA, 11/66 Goulburn Street, Sydney, NSW, 2000; tel: within Australia 1800 066 844 toll free; outside Australia 61 2 9394 7600; fax: 61 2 9394 7601; email: info@copyright.com.au

COPYING FOR OTHER PURPOSES

Except as permitted under the Act, for example a fair dealing for the purposes of study, research, criticism or review, no part of this book may be reproduced, stored in a retrieval system, or transmitted in any form or by any means without prior written permission. All enquiries should be made to the publisher at the address above.

Any performance or public reading of *How to Vote* is forbidden unless a licence has been received from the author or the author's agent. The purchase of this book in no way gives the purchaser the right to perform the play in public, whether by means of a staged production or a reading. All applications for public performance should be addressed to Aurora Artists Management, 51 Egan Street, Newtown, NSW 2042; justine@auroraartists.com

Typeset by Brighton Gray for Currency Press.
Cover shows, L-R: Martha Russell, Charlotte Palmer and Jack Taylor.
Cover photography: Adam McGrath / Hcreations.

Currency Press acknowledges the Traditional Owners of the Country on which we live and work. We pay our respects to all Aboriginal and Torres Strait Islander Elders, past and present.

A catalogue record for this book is available from the National Library of Australia

Contents

HOW TO VOTE
Or, the Repercussions of Political Ambition and Personal Rivalries within Student Leadership and Media Organisations in the Context of the Post-COVID-19 Neoliberal University Institution

Act One	1
Act Two	24
Act Three	57
Act Four	81

Theatre Program at the end of the playtext

How To Vote! was commissioned and first produced by Canberra Youth Theatre at The Playhouse, Canberra Theatre Centre, on 7 September 2022, with the following cast:

VICE-CHANCELLOR	Tracy Noble
TASH	Joanna Richards
PRATCHETT	Claire Imlach
LIZZIE	Caitlin Baker
GILES	Matt White
MON	Ella Buckley
WARREN	Nicholas Bermingham
PHILLIPA	Jasmine Atkins
HANYA	Rahel Alemseged
KEV	Tim Cusack
FIGARO	Jack Shanahan
ELISE	Thea Jade
ANDY	Mischa Rippon
RON	Blue Hyslop
STEW	Callum Doherty
GERT	Martha Russell
ENSEMBLE	

Ashleigh Butler, Jessica Gooding, Quinn Goodwin, Breanna Kelly, Abigail Marceau, Yvette Mpinga, Ben O'Loughlin, Cameron Rose, Emily Smith, Saar Weston

Director, Luke Rogers
Lighting Designer, Antony Hateley
Costume Designer, Helen Wojtas
Sound Designer, Patrick Haesler
Video Designer, Ethan Hamill
Assistant Director, Sophie Tallis
Stage Manager, Rhiley Winnett
Assistant Stage Manager, Ashley Pope
Costume Assistant, Rhiannon Roberts

CHARACTERS

VICE-CHANCELLOR
TASH, fourth year, female
PRATCHETT, fourth year, female

The Sharehouse
LIZZIE, third year, female
KEV, third year, male
PHILLIPA, fourth year, female

The College
GILES, third year, male
WARREN, fourth year, male
HANYA, third year, female

Townies
MON, first year, female

The Alarum Newspaper
FIGARO, third year, male
ELISE, second year, female
ANDY, fourth year, male

The Student Drama Society
RON, third year, male
STEW, third year, male

Miscellaneous
GERT, third year, female
SALLY, gym owner, female
SPARROW, ace hacker, ?

BAAL2001, virtual (the 2001 refers to the birth year of the character so should reflect whatever makes the character 21 at time of production)

OPUSMAGNUM, a virtual alter-ego

SETTING/TIME

In and around a university campus in the winter months. Now-ish.

NOTE ON CASTING

The casting of performers from diverse backgrounds is crucial to the realisation of this work.

The name, backgrounds, gender, sexuality or ability of characters can be changed to reflect those of the performer.

NOTES ON INTERVAL

When the audience leave the theatre for interval, they should be met by a sea of campaigning—the foyer space should be filled with posters, corflutes and A-frames, with spare cast members handing out how-to-vote pamphlets.

Amongst this, you should gather two things:

1) A poll of who the audience would vote for at this stage of the campaign (the results of which will be read out by the celebrity guest in Act Three).

2) A question for GILES and a question for MONICA (these will be asked by the audience member or by FIGARO in the Q&A section in Act Three).

This play text went to press before the end of rehearsals and may differ from the play as performed.

PREFACE

TASH *appears, wearing a dressing gown, a hospital wristband and slippers.*

TASH: When I was younger I wanted to visit my mum at work.

She worked at Parliament House and I spent my formative years sitting at the kitchen table listening to her talk about a minister who said this, or a secretary who did that. It was exciting how many people she simply met in her day. So I started bugging her about visiting the place. The place where all these interesting people were.

Eventually, she let me drop in for the hour and a half between me finishing school and her finishing work. It was meant to stop me from nagging, but it only fed my obsession. I was now *in* the place where all the interesting people were.

Soon dropping by after school became dropping in *before* school, became spending my entire school holidays there doing odd jobs around the place. Imagine it, there's me in a school uniform running around the corridors of power—*being* one of the interesting people.

I gobbled it all up: I learned all the names of all the ministers, electorates, secretaries, secretariats, and even research officers. I bathed in the policies, the rivalries, the scuffles, the histories, the drama!

Then one day, I'm sitting in the House of Reps—by this stage, no biggie at all. Mum's talking to the treasurer, when a voice from behind asks me a question.

'What are you going to do when you grow up?'

I turn around quickly, ready to deploy my trademark sass and attitude, and it's the bloody PM.

Did I freeze? No.

Did I blink? Not a chance.

Without hesitation, I say 'When I grow up I want your job.'

Pause. She puts her hands on her hips.

They piss themselves laughing. I'm not sure what's so funny so I shrug it off but before I know it I'm out of my seat, up the stairs and I feel a pain in my ear and I'm on my arse?

Mum's dragged me out of Question Time and is staring down at me.

'Why do you think I brought you here?'

Because I nagged—

'Why do you think I brought you here?'

Because you wanted to show me how great this place was?

She visibly shuddered.

'The opposite! I wanted to show you how disgusting and awful this place is and how you should do everything in your power to do something else with your life.'

Well—too late, Mum. I'm addicted.

She holds up her hospital wristband.

I'm sick. I don't need to be diagnosed because I've got all the symptoms, and I know no amount of medicine or bed-rest is going to help me to get better or stop me from getting what I want.

Getting more of what I want.

Getting *all* of what I want.

Power.

TASH *smiles.*

Real power.

PRATCHETT *passes her a shovel.*

Thank you, babe.

She digs into the earth with her shovel then walks off.

FIGARO *walks on, wearing with a photojournalist vest and John Lennon glasses, and rolling a cigarette.*

A moment or two passes before the VICE-CHANCELLOR *enters, with a jumbo juice and a straw.*

FIGARO: Evening Vice-Chancellor.
VICE-CHANCELLOR: Evening.
FIGARO: Nice night.
VICE-CHANCELLOR: It is.
FIGARO: Nice night. For a juice.

Beat. FIGARO *pulls out his phone with camera ready.*

VICE-CHANCELLOR: Fuck.

PREFACE

As the VICE-CHANCELLOR *turns around,* FIGARO *has caught a snap.*

FIGARO: Brilliant.
VICE-CHANCELLOR: I'm not on campus.
FIGARO: Is that your quote?
VICE-CHANCELLOR: I'm not giving you a quote because this never happened.
FIGARO: Photo begs to differ.
VICE-CHANCELLOR: Off the record, everything I'm saying is off the record.
FIGARO: A source close to the Vice-Chancellor said 'She was not on campus so it's alright that she's a hypocrite.'
VICE-CHANCELLOR: I stand by the straw ban and though its impact be relatively slight, with due respect to our turtle brothers and sisters, the campaign I led was about raising environmental awareness and I'm proud of what it achieved and what it will achieve.
FIGARO: And this photograph on the front of the newspaper will raise awareness about how much your words really mean.
VICE-CHANCELLOR: Student.
FIGARO: Sorry?
VICE-CHANCELLOR: Front of the *student* newspaper. Look at you with your war-correspondent vest, what's even in the pockets?
FIGARO: Treats. This stake-out took longer than I thought.
VICE-CHANCELLOR: They do food in there.
FIGARO: The cacao and coconut protein balls hurt my tum-tum.
VICE-CHANCELLOR: So how much will it cost to keep this quiet?
FIGARO: Are you suggesting a bribe?
VICE-CHANCELLOR: Off the record.
FIGARO: 'A source close to the Vice-Chancellor suggested a bribe.'
VICE-CHANCELLOR: I'll buy you a juice.

FIGARO *pulls out a metal straw from one of his vest pockets.*

Metal straw?
FIGARO: First rule of a stake-out: Always be prepared for a reverse entrapment.

FIGARO*'s phone beeps, he pulls it out.*

VICE-CHANCELLOR: If I buy you a juice and a snack bar, will you delete the picture?

FIGARO: I'd rather hold on to the photo until I need it.

VICE-CHANCELLOR: 'A source close to the imprisoned student journalist said he is feeling chipper in his cell after blackmailing the high-ranking university official.'

FIGARO: I haven't blackmailed you. Yet.

> FIGARO *is still staring at his phone.*

VICE-CHANCELLOR: Something more pressing?

FIGARO: Yes.

> FIGARO *smiles.*

Ball's in my court, VC. Chat soon.

> FIGARO *runs off. Moment. The* VICE-CHANCELLOR *sips.*

VICE-CHANCELLOR: Worth it for the watermelon.

ACT ONE: THE NOMINATION

1.

Dawn.

The main thoroughfare of the university, overlooked by a looming bell tower.

As the sun rises, we see the place come to life.

Groundskeepers mow and rake.

Cleaners pick up the detritus of the previous day: coffee cups, kebab wrappers, beer bottles.

The place is becoming fresh then ...

Students appear.

Satchel-wearers, backpackers, glasses, cool haircuts, but students all scurrying,

then the athletes,

then the musicians,

then the protesters,

then the counter-protesters,

the dropkicks,

the academics,

the dreamers,

the lovers,

the whole world in symphony.

Then just as quickly everyone vanishes except for ...

2.

The common room of Giles's college. WARREN, *wearing a monk's robe, drinks straight from a whiskey bottle, and* HANYA *plays on her phone.*

The loungeroom of Lizzie's sharehouse. PHILLIPA *and* KEV *pass an eye drop and vial back and forth whilst doing a puzzle.*

HANYA: Should I ask about the robe?
WARREN: I've got a meeting after this.
HANYA: Are you doing that weird soggy Sao shit again?
WARREN: You cum on one biscuit and suddenly that's all you're known for.
HANYA: When you've probably cum on lots of inanimate objects in your time.
WARREN: Exactly.
HANYA: We need music, the suspense is killing me.
WARREN: It's probably not what we're thinking.
HANYA: What are you thinking?
WARREN: All I'm saying is Madam President works in mysterious ways.
HANYA: I didn't know you guys knew each other.
WARREN: Of course we know each other, we're both—
HANYA: Don't say BNOCs.
WARREN: You'll change your spots when you get labelled one.
HANYA: When I'm a big name on campus, I won't use the acronym.
WARREN: My point is Giles is a nice guy but is he up for this?

> WARREN *shrugs and* HANYA *scrolls through a music app.*

KEV: I honestly thought it would do more.
PHILLIPA: What were you expecting, country boy?
KEV: Magic eye puzzle on THC oil?
PHILLIPA: You wanted access to some greater truth?
KEV: I thought you'd get a buzz? You know like when you lick a tractor battery?
PHILLIPA: Not a lot to do growing up on a potato farm is there?
KEV: Do you think music would help?
PHILLIPA: We could try ABC Jazz? I lucid dreamed my way to an HD on Jung last semester.
KEV: What about ABC Country?
PHILLIPA: Men singing about trucks and beer? Hard pass.
KEV: There are female country singers.
PHILLIPA: What do they sing about?
KEV: Killing their husbands.
PHILLIPA: I'm going to keep that in mind but for now I'm going to Spotify 'druggy', 'magic eye', 'transcendental' and … 'luck'

KEV: Luck?

PHILLIPA: Our poor little Lizzie is gonna need every little bit of it.

> WARREN *finishes his bottle and* PHILLIPA *gets up to look at the puzzle from a different angle. In both locations the same song comes on: it's funky, it's smooth, it speaks to them all in a very specific way. They sway, they groove, it's a lot.*
>
> GILES *enters the common room.*
>
> LIZZIE *enters the living room.*

LIZZIE/GILES: Well …

> *They stop dancing, they stop the music.*

WARREN: Spill it.

PHILLIPA: What did she say?

LIZZIE/GILES: You're looking at the new student council president.

> HANYA *hugs* GILES, KEV *hugs* LIZZIE. *They turn on the music again.*
>
> PHILLIPA *and* WARREN *sulk in the corner.*

3.

A forest on the edge of campus.

In a chair next to a fire sits TASH. *She wears a cardigan, jeans and a vintage T-shirt, and types furiously on a laptop.*

PRATCHETT *arrives with* FIGARO, *who has a blindfold over his eyes.*

TASH *stops typing and smiles at* PRATCHETT.

FIGARO: You're the what? P.A.? Bodyguard?

PRATCHETT: Girlfriend. So yeah.

FIGARO: Still at uni?

PRATCHETT: Graduated last year. I'm a consultant.

FIGARO: Sign of a genius, you know?

PRATCHETT: Consulting?

FIGARO: No. Comfortably holding two contradictory thoughts at once like that.

PRATCHETT: Which are?

FIGARO: One: I have just graduated university, two: this entitles me to advise people.

Pause.

PRATCHETT: Do people hate you because you're a dickhead or are you a dickhead because people hate you?
FIGARO: Schrödinger's chicken and egg right there.

PRATCHETT *lets go of* FIGARO *and goes to* TASH.

PRATCHETT: This is it, okay?
TASH: Thanks love.
PRATCHETT: Seriously, after this you need to get back to thesis land.
TASH: Why did you build such an inviting fire then?
PRATCHETT: Because you look cute by firelight.
TASH: I'm very Folklore at the moment.
FIGARO: I could come back if you two—
TASH: Sit down.
PRATCHETT: Last one, okay?
TASH: Pinky promise.

PRATCHETT *and* TASH *pinky promise with a kiss to seal it.* PRATCHETT *undoes the blindfold and stands back and puts on her headphones.*

FIGARO: It was you who gave me the VC juice tip-off.
TASH: Wanted you to know I mean business.
FIGARO: I already knew Tash Bridgers meant business.
TASH: In the flesh.
FIGARO: Head of the O-week committee, student representative to the university board, UN Women representative, student journalist of the year, national debating champion, secretary of the jazz society, emeritus president of the cheese club, current president of the student council with no signs of stopping for breath before breezing into a second term … and you're not running again.
TASH: What?
FIGARO: That came to me just now but makes sense actually.
TASH: How?
FIGARO: Well you posted an Instagram story that you were taking a bit of time off socials to deal with a family matter, but you've clearly had a mental breakdown.

TASH: How'd you reach that point?
FIGARO: You're sitting by a fire in a forest on the edge of campus, your loving yet weirdly intimidating partner is monitoring your workload, plus you've still got a hospital bracelet on from a private hospital that deals exclusively with eating disorders and mental breakdowns.
TASH: Maybe I have bulimia?
FIGARO: You *are* wearing a baggy cardigan but the Tay Tay reference just before makes me think that's a choice not a shield, so flip of the coin really. Tell me Tash, do you hate your body?

    TASH *claps.*

TASH: Wow.
FIGARO: Who's your successor?
TASH: Straight for the jugular.
FIGARO: You wouldn't be considering stepping down from the throne if you didn't know who was going to pick up the sceptre.
TASH: I'll be keeping the crown, goes well with my highlights.
FIGARO: So …
TASH: I've picked a few successors actually.
FIGARO: Spicy.
TASH: What do you think?
FIGARO: You tell me their names and I'll tell you whether you made the right choice.
TASH: I wasn't talking to you.

    PRATCHETT *takes off the headphones.*

PRATCHETT: He went full Mind Palace.
FIGARO: Rude. Listening in on others' conversations.
PRATCHETT: Nothing playing.
TASH: Think he's the right choice—not one of the more junior reporters?
PRATCHETT: Oh totally perfect.
FIGARO: What do you want with me?
PRATCHETT: She wants a stooge.
TASH: Babe. Don't be so crude. I need a … stooge.
FIGARO: I'm an independent operator.
TASH: Everyone is until I ask them this question … What's your wildest dream?

FIGARO: Why?
TASH: I'm going to give it to you on a silver platter.

4.

LIZZIE, *as Brutus, dressed in Roman garb, opposite* STEW, *in theatre blacks.*

LIZZIE: I prithee, Strato, stay thou by thy lord:
Thou art a fellow of a good respect;
Thy life hath had some smatch of honour in it:
Hold then my sword, and turn away thy face,
While I do run upon it. Wilt thou, Strato?

STEW, *much more wooden.*

STEW: Give me your hand first.
Fare you well, my lord.

LIZZIE *unsheathes a sword from her belt and passes it to* STEW.

LIZZIE: Farewell, good Strato.

Runs on her sword.

Caesar, now be still: I kill'd not thee with half so good a will.

LIZZIE *dies.*

A moment.

STEW *looks up.*

Another moment.

A small trickle of blood falls on her head then stops.

RON: [*off*] And scene!

RON *enters.*

The blood is meant to fall as she falls on her sword.

KEV *enters holding a rope.*

KEV: Yeah I get it but the rope broke.
RON: Remember, when we watched the Ivo Van Hove version on NT Live? The blood's meant to drop as soon as she falls on her sword.
KEV: Yeah I get it but the rope broke.

ACT ONE

RON: It's meant to be shocking, it's meant to be real, it's meant to be hyper-real.

KEV: Bro!

KEV walks off.

LIZZIE: I think the rope broke, dear.

RON: Oh.

LIZZIE: Can I get a towel?

RON: That blood needs to drop every single death.

STEW: That's a lot of death, Ron.

RON: It's Julius Caesar, *Stew*.

STEW: Yeah but he dies like halfway through.

RON: It's because Shakespeare drew people in with the big name then blammo kills him early and they're like 'whaaaa?' Ruffs blowing off, Elizabethan panties dropping.

STEW: Your articulacy amazes me sometimes.

RON: I amaze myself all the time.

LIZZIE: Ron, would you mind if we wrapped there for the day?

RON: For you my dear Brutus—anything. That's a wrap, guys. We'll pick up from the top tomorrow. And if anybody sees Kev, could we try and find out what happened with the blood?

STEW picks up his bag.

Practise your iambic, Stew.

STEW: I'm the costume designer.

RON: You're also Strato.

STEW: Which is that one scene.

RON: And I don't want your one scene to ruin my production. Come on now. Beat it out on your chest: de-dum de-dum de-dum de-dum de-dum.

STEW leaves.

You've got a secret.

LIZZIE: I do not.

RON: You've been distracted all rehearsal.

LIZZIE: I've got someone on my mind.

RON: Are you seeing someone else?

LIZZIE: I am not.

RON: Did you kiss someone else?
LIZZIE: I wanted to.
RON: You're opening up to my proposal then?
LIZZIE: Not like that. In the 'I could kiss you' way.
RON: Who's the lucky lady?
LIZZIE: Tash Bridgers.
RON: Very attractive woman.
LIZZIE: Really?
RON: I'm attracted to power.
LIZZIE: Well …

> LIZZIE *sits and drags* RON *to the ground.*

RON: Well …

> RON *beats a drum roll on his legs.*

LIZZIE: Tash is not running for a second year as president and she wants me to run instead.

> *Pause.* RON *stands up and begins pacing.*

RON: She's not running?
LIZZIE: No.
RON: And she wants you to run?
LIZZIE: Yes.
RON: Why?
LIZZIE: She said that because of how many people saw my *Mao's Last Dancer* and through my work with the revues and the campus bake sales and the—wait, what do you mean?
RON: Why did she ask you?
LIZZIE: I just told you.
RON: I know, I know but …
LIZZIE: Why didn't she ask you?
RON: Your words, not mine, but yeah. Why didn't she ask me?
LIZZIE: Oh. Maybe she tried to reach you and—
RON: I'm too busy anyway.
LIZZIE: Totally.
RON: I've got my NIDA audition coming up.
LIZZIE: Totally.
RON: And my show.

LIZZIE: *Our* show.
RON: Ha, sure.
LIZZIE: We've been planning this for years.
RON: Well I had the idea in high school but sure, whatever—up and leave.
LIZZIE: I don't want to.
RON: Well you've clearly chosen Tash over me so …
LIZZIE: But I love our Brutus. We've built her together.
RON: I'll see if Stew wants to take it on. He'll be terrible and everything will be ruined but you've left me with no choice so thanks for that.

> RON *picks up* LIZZIE*'s script and puts it in her bag then passes her the bag.*

LIZZIE: We're talking.
RON: I'm giving you time.
LIZZIE: We need to talk about this.
RON: And I need to finish painting *our* set.
LIZZIE: It's already painted.
RON: It's something you've never been able to grasp about the theatre: things need layers.

5.

A candle-lit room. A man in a hooded robe walks forward.

WARREN: Men are under attack.

> *Two more men walk forward in hooded robes intoning …*

HOODED MEN: Dori me
>> Interimo adapare, dori me

WARREN: From feminists, cancel culture and unrealistic body expectations.
HOODED MEN: Ameno, ameno, latire
>> Latiremo, dori me
>> Ameno
>> Omenare imperavi ameno
>> Dimere, dimere mantiro
>> Mantiremo, ameno

> *Two men enter either end of the hallway in their boxer shorts, shivering.*

WARREN: We must learn to defend ourselves against this metaphysical onslaught.

HOODED MEN: Omenare imperavi emulari, ameno
Omenare imperavi emulari, ameno.

WARREN: Welcome to … Murder Ball.

Two more men walk forward in hooded robes holding an exercise ball each. They pass one to each of the men in boxer shorts.

The rules are simple. Run as hard and as fast as you possibly can at each other. If you go puss, you disgrace your gender. If you slow down, you disgrace your gender.

WARREN *taps one of the hooded men who then passes each of the men in their boxers a can of beer.*

If you don't sink your piss before you begin, you disgrace your gender.

The two men in boxer shorts shotgun their beers. A phone beeps.

Who the fuck was that?

No-one answers. The phone rings.

GILES: If it rings twice then it gets rid of the Do Not Disturb, you know that!

One of the hooded men turns on the lights. We're actually in Giles's college room.

Sorry mate, it's Gert—we get like half an hour where our schedules sync up.

WARREN: Moving this to my bedroom. Bring the beer, bring the balls.

GILES *grabs a can of beer and an exercise ball and sits on it. Everyone else leaves.*

GERT*'s face is projected. She's on FaceTime.*

GILES: Where are you?

GERT: Hampstead Heath. Isn't it beautiful?

GERT *starts moving—we see a forest behind her.*

GILES: You always wanted to go there.

GERT: I always wanted to come here with you!

GILES: Maybe I'm right behind you—oooOOoooh!

ACT ONE

GERT: Are you drinking Gi-Guy?

> GILES *holds up his beer can.*

GILES: Nah, it's a prop.
GERT: Are you in a play?
GILES: Started a podcast.
GERT: What's it called?
GILES: This Guy Had A Big Dayyyyyyyyy.
GERT: Needs a snappier title.
GILES: Did you hear what I said?
GERT: Yeah you've got a visual prop for your audio podcast.
GILES: The title of the show, Gert.
GERT: I'm sorry, you're cutting out—what are you saying?
GILES: I had a big day.
GERT: You're hammered.
GILES: And you're in fucking England, don't hear me going on about it.
GERT: You'll be here soon.
GILES: Maybe.
GERT: Maybe?
GILES: Enjoy the Heath!
GERT: Not as much as if you were here.
GILES: Miss you baby.
GERT: Love you baby.

> GILES *hangs up, lies on his back.*

GILES: Moved halfway around the world to avoid me baby.

> *He then pours the rest of the beer into his mouth in a beautiful arch until there's none left.*

Giles, you're a schmuck.

> GILES *takes off his shirt.*

Giles, you're a drunk schmuck.

> GILES *takes off his shorts.*

Giles, you're a drunk schmuck who's fucked.

> GILES *jumps into bed in his undies.*
>
> *He downloads an app, waits for it to load then puts his phone onto charge.*

The message tone sounds.
He rolls over.
The message tone sounds again.
He rolls onto his back staring at the ceiling.
He picks up his phone and deletes the app then rolls over.

6.

The corridor outside the Vice-Chancellor's office.
LIZZIE, *with a Gatorade, tries desperately to get the fake blood out of her hair.*
GILES *walks in, still in his robe, and carrying a Gatorade.*
They're both very hungover.

GILES: Are you—
LIZZIE: What?
GILES: Okay? It looks pretty bad. Your head.
LIZZIE: Oh.
GILES: I don't think it should be bleeding that much.
LIZZIE: It's fake.
GILES: Oh.
LIZZIE: I'm an actor.
GILES: Oh.

    Pause.

LIZZIE: Long out of the seminary?
GILES: Huh?
LIZZIE: The robe?
GILES: Oh. It's fake too.
LIZZIE: Costume party?
GILES: Kind of hey.
LIZZIE: I'm Lizzie.
GILES: Giles.
LIZZIE: Big night?
GILES: Could ask the same of you.
LIZZIE: Need my electrolytes. I just went for a run.

GILES: Where?
LIZZIE: Around … the … track.
GILES: Convincing.

> LIZZIE *and* GILES *cheers with their Gatorades.*

LIZZIE: You getting expelled?
GILES: Don't think so.
LIZZIE: Decided to nurse a hangover outside the Vice-Chancellor's office then?
GILES: My name's Giles O'Hagan and I'm running for student president.
LIZZIE: Wow.
GILES: That sounded so weird.
LIZZIE: Sounded like you've practised it.
GILES: This morning in the mirror.
LIZZIE: In between voms?
GILES: In between voms, yes.
LIZZIE: Well congratulations.
GILES: I haven't won yet.
LIZZIE: I meant on the nomination but look at that little grin of yours, you think you've got this in the bag—don't you?
GILES: Like, I don't want to seem arrogant but I'm running unopposed.
LIZZIE: No-one else threw their hat in the ring, huh?
GILES: Not that I know.

> *Beat.*

LIZZIE: You should add me. On Insta.
GILES: Oh. Sorry. I've got a girlfriend.
LIZZIE: Um, I just want your robe! My dream production, like dreeeeeam production is *R&J*, I've got it all sketched out, but this isn't your straight-arse bloodless Nazi-makes-it-relevant Shakespeare, oh no: punk it up a bit, queer it around the edges, lots of dance, lots of microphones, very Berlin. Keep the priest though, chaps and robes. The prince as Gaga at the Met Ball sort of vibe. You know?
GILES: Not really. No.

> VICE-CHANCELLOR *arrives.*

VICE-CHANCELLOR: Giles?
GILES: Yes.

VICE-CHANCELLOR: I'm not going to bother with the robe.
GILES: Thank you.
VICE-CHANCELLOR: You can come in.
GILES: Nice to meet you, Lizzie.
VICE-CHANCELLOR: Elizabeth, you too.

    GILES*'s smiles fades.*

LIZZIE: Oops.

7.

The VICE-CHANCELLOR *enters with* LIZZIE *and* GILES. *She motions for them to take a seat in the lounge area.*

MON, *in a moon boot, is in front of the* VICE-CHANCELLOR*'s desk. The* VICE-CHANCELLOR *sits behind it.*

FIGARO *is in the corner with a camera around his neck, nodding occasionally.*

MON: —in New Caledonia there's the Napoleonic system still so we have to listen to teachers, listen to them and that's it, never question them because they teach from a place of knowledge and we learn from a place of ignorance so that was my entire primary school and my entire high school oh and jumping back my pre-school even and when I started learning a bit more about it and how it wasn't the only system it wasn't even the best system in the world it was just the one that they had in New Caledonia, France—obvs, parts of Algeria, parts of Benin and Vietnam but they probably don't want to talk about that because of the whole colonial angle and France more than any other country doesn't want to talk about that because that's more of a British thing, an India thing, a white-man's burden thing and anyway when I moved from there to here I was already ready, I was ready already for the switch to the different learning system where you could question your teachers, where you could go 'hey, I don't think so Kevo' and it was allowed, not accepted but allowed, not allowed but encouraged and here I am talking back and I feel like I'm learning I feel like I'm growing and then BAM brick wall baby BRICK WALL hits me because I realise that talking back might be encouraged but it's limited, it's within parameters, it's within a schema, a broader way of thinking of not talking back so now I realise that I'm not a free range chicken, I'm a cage chicken, like I'm grateful that I'm not a battery hen but I'm still in a cage you know so when I came in this morning and I told your secretary about the hole, the hole did she tell you about the hole, about the hole out the front of my bus stop and I am here on behalf of all the students who catch that bus because I was chosen to speak because I am often one to speak and I was told that you were the person to talk to and I had to not talk to her anymore because her ears were bleeding and they weren't bleeding they were just like she was just you know it was a metaphor or an analogy or a—oh PONDICHERRY is another example of a place outside of France that has the Napoleonic system so yeah.

Pause.

VICE-CHANCELLOR: This is Mon.

MON *waves.*

Mon's been here for—

FIGARO: About two hours now.

MON: I … yeah sorry once I get started speaking I find it hard to stop.

VICE-CHANCELLOR: So, there's a hole at your bus stop?

MON: There's a lot more wrong with it than a hole.

VICE-CHANCELLOR: But you trod in a hole?

MON: And I broke my ankle, yes.

VICE-CHANCELLOR: That's unfortunate. When was this?

MON: A few Tuesdays ago.

VICE-CHANCELLOR: What time of day did the incident occur, dear?

MON: I don't know. About ten o'clock.

VICE-CHANCELLOR: Okay so bus stops on campus when classes are in session are not actually a university issue, they are a student council issue. I would be the person who could solve this for you if it were a few hours earlier but unfortunately it's out of my hands.

MON: It's the same bus stop?

VICE-CHANCELLOR: Welcome to the world of university bureaucracy. Is it tedious? Yes. Is it effective? No.

MON: So who's in charge of the student council? Who do I talk to?

VICE-CHANCELLOR: It's in caretaker mode until the next election.

MON: Who's in the next election?

VICE-CHANCELLOR: That's what these lovely people are here to talk about.

    LIZZIE *and* GILES *smile at* MON.

I hope that clears things up—
MON: I can wait.
VICE-CHANCELLOR: I've got other meetings after this—
MON: I'm sure they'll want this cleared up as quickly as you, it would be a real shame if a public liability class action suit were to be filed—I don't know how many people that hole has affected but I'm sure I can find out, would you like me to go find that out for you while you talk to these nice people?
VICE-CHANCELLOR: I'll be right with you.

    MON *gets out her phone and starts tapping madly.*

Okay then. Take a seat.

    The VICE-CHANCELLOR *moves to the lounge area.*

Well this is exciting, isn't it? As you probably both know, but I'm legally obliged to give this spiel, the student council president is a very prestigious and important job—the title is twofold: yes, it's a political position—you are elected by the students, for the students, from the students—you are their mouthpiece to, their standard-bearer for, their shield from, the outside world. But it is also a corporate position—you are the head of a company with an annual turnover of thirty million dollars a year, which delivers everything on campus that is not academic. This is a fun job, this is a big job, this is a difficult job, one that the founders of this university over a hundred and sixty years ago deemed so important that it should be given to a student on a yearly elected basis with no direct supervision.

    The VICE-CHANCELLOR *lets a big breath out.*

But don't let that spook you, I was expecting this to be a one-horse race. Any clue on what happened to Tash Bridgers? I assumed I'd be seeing only her today.
GILES: She decided not to run.
LIZZIE: Family stuff.

    GILES *looks at* LIZZIE—*what does she know?*
Apparently.

VICE-CHANCELLOR: Well I can't say no to a good duel. Have you two met?

GILES: Briefly.

LIZZIE: Outside, just now.

VICE-CHANCELLOR: Well I'm sure you're both nice people so this will go swimmingly. You're both third years?

> *They nod.*

So you've been through this as spectators a couple of times already.

MON: I'm in first year, I wouldn't mind—

VICE-CHANCELLOR: From today, it's a month until election day. You've got the debate in three weeks. Due to the new environmental regulations on campus—physical campaign materials re: posters, pamphlets, placards—are strictly limited to the week leading up to the election.

FIGARO: Fuck them straws, right VC?

VICE-CHANCELLOR: Quite. But we're not old fashioned, internet campaigning can occur within university guidelines of course. We take information security very seriously on this campus. Any questions on the digital front?

> *They shake their heads.*

For everything your campaign requires, you have a budget of *one* thousand dollars. Stick to it or be bounced—don't try and find ways around it because we will know. That's about it really. Any questions?

MON: I have one.

VICE-CHANCELLOR: I was really hoping you'd melted into the floor by now.

MON: How do you get nominated?

VICE-CHANCELLOR: We're just getting to that.

> *The* VICE-CHANCELLOR *opens a drawer and passes out nomination forms to* GILES *and* LIZZIE.

Initial here.

> *They initial and turn the page.*

Initial there.

They initial and turn the page.

Sign and date there.

They sign and date.

Witness each other.

They switch forms and sign and date.

Congratulations you two.

The VICE-CHANCELLOR *takes the forms back behind her desk and picks up a big rubber stamp.*

With the power vested in me by the students of this—
MON: I would like to run.
VICE-CHANCELLOR: Why?
MON: To fill the hole.
VICE-CHANCELLOR: To fill the hole?
MON: To fill the hole.
VICE-CHANCELLOR: Well, I've had less inspiring candidates.

The VICE-CHANCELLOR *passes a form to* MON.

Initial here.

MON *initials and turns the page.*

Initial there.

MON *initials and turns the page.*

Sign and date there.

She signs and dates.

Can I get a witness?

GILES *and* LIZZIE *don't move.* FIGARO *steps forward and signs and dates it.*

The VICE-CHANCELLOR *stamps all three forms with a flourish.*

Congratulations you *three.* May the odds be ever in your favour.

Beat.

My kids like the books, I think the movies are better personally.

Beat.

Don't kill each other. Please.

FIGARO: Quick photo of the three of you.

>LIZZIE, GILES *and* MON *stand in the corner.*
>
>*They take a photo.*
>
>*This is splashed against the back of the stage.*

ACT TWO: THE CAMPAIGN

1.

The office of the student newspaper.
ELISE *and* ANDY *are at the table.*

ELISE: Can you cover the women's rugby?
ANDY: I'm already covering archery.
ELISE: You're covering *men's* archery.
ANDY: I just said that.
ELISE: You need to say the men's, not just assume it.
ANDY: Why do you have to make everything about gender?
ELISE: Because everything is about gender.
ANDY: I don't see gender.
ELISE: Please jump back into your alt-right box before I flip a table.
ANDY: I don't see how that makes me a bigot. Perhaps you and the Reddit forum you stole your ideas off could mansplain it to me?
ELISE: Why are you allowed to keep saying stuff like this every meeting?
ANDY: Because I'm the only one who understands sports and sports is the only bit of the paper people read.
ELISE: Incorrect.
ANDY: Ahem, biggest *digital* imprint.
ELISE: We are primarily a print newspaper.

    FIGARO *enters.*

People pick us up between classes, they might flick through an article if they know the person who wrote it or who is in it, hence the social pages are the only pages people really care about—Figaro, back me up.
FIGARO: I couldn't possibly care any less about what either of you were talking about. The student election season is upon us and from this issue on, it's going to be filling every single page of ours.
ANDY: What happened to straw-gate?
ELISE: Weren't you going to blow it wide open?

ANDY: You said you had a source.
ELISE: You said you had a Spiro Agnew!
ANDY: Which I had to look up.
FIGARO: We've moved on, this is going to be massive.
ANDY: How? It's already sewn up.
ELISE: Tash has it in the bag.
ANDY: Ever since Tash Bridgers got her ATAR results, she's been running for president.
ELISE: Her tactical placement within the college system and strong extracurricular activities means she sweeps the board.
FIGARO: I know this, you know this, who is this for?
ANDY: I wanted to make sure we were all on the same page.
ELISE: And why there was no point covering this election because it's already sewn up.
ANDY: Tash has it in the bag.
FIGARO: Hold on to your butts. For reasons unknown, Tash Bridgers has decided not to run for a second term.
ANDY/ELISE: What?!

FIGARO rummages through a pile of junk on the desk and brings out a manila folder.

ANDY: Did you know this and not tell me?
ELISE: I didn't know this.
FIGARO: Thank you everyone.
ANDY: If you're hiding shit because of the gender stuff?
FIGARO: If I could get a bit of hush, thank you.
ELISE: I didn't fucking know.
FIGARO: FUCKING SHUT UP!

A hush falls.

Precisely because of what just happened, I've made an editorial call. Anything and everything to do with this election will run through and be written by our new election correspondent. Namely, me.

There's muted applause to say the least.

Amongst the regular fast-train, free-pot, lemonade-in-the-bubblers policies floating around for the student council, the race for president is unprecedented on a number of levels: firstly, this is the first three-way race in the last hundred-odd years, secondly, the spread and calibre of the candidates means this election is going to be very difficult to predict, thirdly ... there isn't a third, I just work in threes, it's a verbal tic.

> FIGARO *opens up the folder: he brings out a headshot of Giles and holds it up—*

Candidate one: Giles O'Hagan.

> GILES *appears.*

Prototypical Abercrombie and Fitch fraternity law-school bro. Dad was mayor of a major city, his mum runs a charity that helps dogs get school uniforms in rogue states. He's got two younger brothers with names that wouldn't seem out of place in an upper-class dog park. Private-school educated, rugger-minded. Girlfriend—Gert—is a bigwig at the women's college and is currently on exchange at LSE because clichés are cheaper by the dozen.

ELISE: Who's running him?

> WARREN *appears beside* GILES.

FIGARO: The Machiavelli of the O'Hagan campaign is Warren Moran—of the great construction dynasty. He's the student politics version of an angler fish—bottom-dweller, sharp teeth.

ELISE: Light bulb on his head?

FIGARO: Could be. We don't know what's under that gel.

> HANYA *appears beside* GILES.

Running logistics is Hanya Dasari—college socials secretary for second year in a row and once she finds the poison Anna Wintour is *not* immune to, editor of *Vogue*.

> *Lights down on* GILES, WARREN *and* HANYA.
>
> FIGARO *holds up the headshot of Lizzie.*

Candidate two: Lizzie Somers.

> LIZZIE *appears.*

Progressive poster child. Grew up in a single-parent household, her mum is a senior public servant, she's got one older sister that's studying at Sciences Po. Her name was allegedly picked out of the appendix to Shakespeare's Collected Works. Public-school

ACT TWO   27

educated, selective for high school, free-thinker. Boyfriend—Ron—is president of the student drama society and is currently directing what will probably be the most awful *Julius Caesar* the world has ever seen. Somers's campaign is being led by—

>PHILLIPA *appears beside* LIZZIE.

Phillipa Pullman—rainbow warrior, animal rights activist, social justice warrior, purist, all-around smelly armpit and proud of it.

>KEV *appears beside her.*

With general charm and suspiciously large bicep support from Kev Cook—fresh off the potato truck from south-west Queensland. His country smile will be deployed for strategic effect to people who are still afraid of out-and-out socialism.

ANDY: Spud between the ears that one.
ELISE: Undeniably good kisser though.
ANDY: Totally.

>*Lights out on* LIZZIE, KEV *and* PHILLIPA.

FIGARO: Candidate three is Monica DuPuissant. A real dark horse.

>MON *appears on the road outside her house.*

Wait, did I say dark horse? I meant dead mule. Was educated overseas, no family of note, isn't connected to any groups on campus, lives in town. No base, no race. Seems to be running on a single issue.

ANDY: Which is?
FIGARO: Filling the hole.
ELISE: Is that a sex thing?

>FIGARO *reading from notes.*

FIGARO: There is a hole in the road outside her bus stop—she broke her ankle and she doesn't want it to happen to others.
ANDY: So she's running for student president.
FIGARO: Not running very far is what I'm saying.
ELISE: Because she broke her ankle?
ANDY: Eh?
ELISE: Eh!
ANDY/ELISE: Ehhhhh.

Lights out on MON.

FIGARO: Questions?

ELISE: Do we know why they're running?

ANDY: They're popular kids, right? Popular kids want tiaras?

ELISE: But they're not the *most* popular. The more obvious choice is Warren over Giles, right? He'll either be the future head of the LNP, or he'll run the asbestos lobby.

ANDY: Now that you mention it, I guess I would've pitched Phillipa over Lizzie too. Bigger profile on and off campus.

FIGARO: Maybe that's it? Too much baggage? Worth looking into.

FIGARO *sticks the three headshots on the wall behind him.*

You are the eyes and ears of campus, and I want to know every bloody thing you see, and every bloody thing you hear. I've also set up an anonymous tip line to—

FIGARO *holds up his phone.*

—my number that will hopefully get us a healthy dose of leaks. I will be the nerve centre, the neocortex, the centre of this moral universe, and I will be the judge, jury and—if needed—executioner of these candidates, because it is our duty to make sure that the students of this university make their most informed decision on election day. We are staring down the barrel of a tooth-and-nail sell-your-mother campaign. Make no mistake this will be a game of inches, it will come down to a handful of votes so consider our words worth their weight in printer ink. Now get out there and rake some muck!

ANDY *and* ELISE *start packing up their bags.*

Rake. Some. Muck.

ANDY *and* ELISE *leave quite casually.*

TASH *steps out from somewhere doing a slow clap.*

TASH: Great speech.

FIGARO: Fuck me!

TASH: Maybe later. LOL.

FIGARO: Is this all you do? The cloak-and-dagger routine?

TASH: That and my honours project.

FIGARO: What's it on again?

TASH: Bronze Age collapse.
FIGARO: How … relevant.
TASH: If you only knew.

TASH stares at FIGARO for a moment.

I know nobody likes you but you're growing on me in a weird little way.
FIGARO: Like a crush?
TASH: Like a cyst.
FIGARO: What now? Just cover the election? Never have the stakes been so high for a prize so measley. Three boring people enter, one gets to be the VC's puppet.
TASH: Oh they're far from boring.
FIGARO: An aspiring actress and a college boy. And the 'fill the hole' chick.
TASH: I chose them for their specific brand of volatility.
FIGARO: That being?
TASH: Lizzie sees herself as an underdog, always has been—is driven by proving everyone wrong.
FIGARO: Immovable object.
TASH: Giles grew up with a silver spoon, he assumes everything he does is right and has never questioned anything in his life.
FIGARO: Unstoppable force. What about Mon?
TASH: Outlier. No concern for you.
FIGARO: Outlier? Weirdly *academic* term.

FIGARO gets a phone call.

TASH: Who is it?
FIGARO: Tipline.
TASH: Oh you're not going to need that, my new little friend.

2.

The common room of Giles's college. WARREN *and* HANYA *stand at the front of the room,* GILES *sits next to them on a chair. The room is filled with college kids.*

The loungeroom of Lizzie's sharehouse. PHILLIPA *and* KEV *stand at the front of the room,* LIZZIE *sits next to them on a chair. The room is filled with friends.*

The same blackboard exists in both rooms simultaneously.

WARREN: Brothers.
PHILLIPA: Welcome.
HANYA: Sisters.
KEV: G'day.
WARREN: We are gathered here today with one mission and one mission alone.
PHILLIPA: We are all here today to show our support
WARREN: To get our fellow collegiate Giles O'Hagan,
PHILLIPA: To get our amazing friend Lizzie Somers
WARREN/PHILLIPA: Elected as student council president.
KEV: Stand up Lizzie.
HANYA: Take a bow Giles.

> GILES *and* LIZZIE *stand up and wave.*

WARREN: Warren. Everything on this campaign—every decision, every dollar spent, every word uttered—runs through me, you will be hearing from me first thing in the morning and last thing at night, I will *not* be hearing from you.
PHILLIPA: For those I haven't met yet my name is Phillipa and I'm Lizzie's housemate and campaign manager and I'll be your first port of call for anything and everything campaign related but we'd like to make this as much of a group effort as possible.
HANYA: I'm Hanya, I'll be running on-the-ground engagement, but again just shoot your hand up if there's anything that you think would be great to put out there. Now is everyone good for drinks?
KEV: I'm Kev and I didn't come here to *fuck* around. If Phillipa's the brains, I'm the brawn. If she's the mind, I'm the muscle.

> *He flexes for the group—it's impressive, he gets some applause.*

Anything or anyone needs, I'm your man.
PHILLIPA: Bit much?
KEV: Is everyone right for tea?
WARREN: Introductions done, let's get down to basics.
PHILLIPA: If everyone's good for drinks, maybe we kick off?
WARREN: Hanya?
PHILLIPA: Kev?

> KEV *and* HANYA *take turns illustrating the following.*

ACT TWO 31

WARREN: Broadly the undergraduate vote
PHILLIPA: Can be split in thirds.
WARREN: Group One:
KEV: Sandstone bastions of the university experience.
WARREN: Every time you read an article about the 'leaders of tomorrow' they're talking about members of these groups. The colleges.

A cheer from the college room.

KEV: The sports groups
WARREN: And the debaters.
WARREN/PHILLIPA: Accurately titled:
GILES: The Elites.
KEV: Group two:
PHILLIPA: Comprised of those active in extracurricular activities, student societies and campus life.

A cheer from the lounge room.

HANYA: There are about a hundred and fifty rough groupings around campus.
PHILLIPA: Faculty associations,
HANYA: Social justice causes,
PHILLIPA: Cultural groups,
LIZZIE: Creative arts,
HANYA: Public-speaking groups
KEV/HANYA: Loosely called:
LIZZIE: The Involved.
PHILLIPA: Then you've got the remainder of the population.
WARREN: The division into thirds is a bit of a misnomer.
PHILLIPA: These three pieces are in increasing order.
KEV: But a minority in participation.
HANYA: They are students who live in town,
WARREN: They catch the bus in,
PHILLIPA: They go to class,
KEV: They *might* eat lunch
WARREN: And they catch the bus home
HANYA: To their high-school friends.
KEV: They steer clear of elections and all associated drama

PHILLIPA: Because that is not what they are incurring horrendous student debt to do.

KEV/HANYA: They are:

LIZZIE/GILES: The Wasteland.

>   KEV *stands away from the board.*

PHILLIPA: If that's the electorate, then who will vote for us?

WARREN: We have decided on a strategy built around the base.

>   HANYA *circles 'The Elites'.*

We need to secure eighty percent of these potential voters. Sounds lofty but these are all traditionally solid columns of support.

HANYA: We convince the leaders and the rest will follow, sort of thing.

WARREN: My volunteering on the last election showed us that people want to vote for us, but we just have to be seen to be out and about getting them.

HANYA: When we get all three—

WARREN: It's in the bag.

>   *The college cheers.*

>   HANYA *steps away from the board.*

PHILLIPA: We have decided on a campaign built around the persuadables.

>   KEV *circles 'The Involved'.*

All we need is just over sixty percent of these voters.

KEV: We are seeking to rally those who believe in not what this university was but what it could be. A lot of you know I'm a country boy and this place has opened up my eyes to what is possible and I think that there's a version of this university which is not a corporation—

PHILLIPA: But a family. If my volunteering on the latest election taught me anything, it's important that we are seen not be some disconnected progressive do-gooders, we are not some ivory tower—

KEV: We are a non-denominational country fair of knowledge and growth for all who seek it.

>   *Is* KEV *crying?*

PHILLIPA: This will not be an easy campaign. But we are confident we have the message and the candidate to get us across the line.

>   *The sharehouse cheers.*

ACT TWO

GILES: Now we're not foolish, we're not the only horse in this race.
LIZZIE: There are three candidates running.
GILES: We've decided as a team
LIZZIE: To not focus too much attention on Monica. She's a first year and although we wish her best in the future, for now—
GILES: She's a non-starter.
LIZZIE: At worst a third-party spoiler.
GILES: But we're confident she doesn't have the tools to get too much traction.
LIZZIE/GILES: Our focus is on
LIZZIE: Giles O'Hagan.
GILES: Lizzie Somers.
LIZZIE: We're not expecting anything too crazy out of his HQ—like in most every other avenue in life they'll probably just end up doing what their dad did.
GILES: These gals are going to be a bit more unpredictable.
LIZZIE: Strategy wise: expect a lot of back-room dealing, you scratch my back I'll scratch yours. We won't really know what they're doing until debate day, so we focus on our own ground game until then.
GILES: They are riding a new wave: expect a more eco-friendly campaign, more of a web presence, think AOC meets GetUp with a bit of Borat thrown in for good measure. They are about transparency, change and coalitions.
LIZZIE: They've got an easier job with a lot more resources but they will still be sneaky.
GILES: They've got amazing reach and potential to mobilise it, but that's a very hard job in a month.
LIZZIE/GILES: Any questions?
PHILLIPA: Oh before we forget.
WARREN: One more thing. Hanya, would you mind?
HANYA: Of course.

> HANYA *goes to fetch something.*

PHILLIPA: Kev, if you please?

> KEV *wipes his eyes and nods, he leaves to fetch something.*
>
> HANYA *comes in with a box.*

LIZZIE: That was quick.

GILES: Already?

    WARREN *passes* GILES *a pair of scissors.*

WARREN: Open it up.

    He opens the box and pulls out a T-shirt and holds it up.

    It says 'Giles!' on the front.

HANYA: Put it on.

    KEV *comes back in with an easel with a cloth over it.*

PHILLIPA: Go on.

    LIZZIE *pulls the cloth off the easel.*

    There's a giant poster with her face in profile with the word 'I'm With Lizzie!' next to it.

    GILES *now has the shirt on.*

PHILLIPA/WARREN: Presenting your next student council president.

    Cheers erupt in both the college and the sharehouse.

3.

The student theatre.

RON *up a ladder.* STEW *is holding it.*

RON: I just don't get what that bumpkin did wrong.

STEW: He's very strong, he pulled it and it broke.

RON: Then fucks off.

STEW: I don't know what you want me to do?

RON: Get better rope.

STEW: With what money?

RON: Bell Shakespeare will be watching this show.

STEW: They've heard about it?

RON: Ha. Of course they have. They're scared of it. They want it to fail because if we get this right, it's all over for them. Now, please, can you find some money in the budget or in your wallet for some better bloody rope.

    LIZZIE *enters.*

STEW: Heyyyyyy.

ACT TWO

RON: Ladder Stew.
STEW: I heard about your nomination.
RON: Stew could you please hold the ladder.
STEW: Big stuff. Huge stuff. Hope we can still do our *Romeo and Juliet*.
LIZZIE: Of course we'll do our *Romeo and Juliet*.
STEW: I found some chaps.
LIZZIE: I saw this guy in a robe …
RON: FUCKING LADDER STEWART!
STEW: [*whispering*] This isn't about the ladder.

    LIZZIE *holds the ladder.*

Good luck.

    STEW *leaves.*

RON: I'm not a monster, it's WH&S.

    RON *climbs down the ladder.*

We're barely above code as it is and if an inspector walks in, we're toast—thus ends the longest running tradition in this sandstone hellhole.

    RON *looks at* LIZZIE *before breaking off to pick up something.*

Ironic, huh?
LIZZIE: What?
RON: Much like Caesar, I was too proud to heed the omens.

    RON *turns around wearing a golden wreath as a crown.*

LIZZIE: What omens?
RON: At the very beginning of all this, when I suggested you have an understudy and you said you didn't need one.
LIZZIE: No-one else has one.
RON: Because you're not used to such a big part and I was protecting you.
LIZZIE: What about *Mao's Last Dancer*? I was the lead.
RON: Yeah …
LIZZIE: Yeah …
RON: It was a solo dance thing you did with your girlfriends.
LIZZIE: And what's this?
RON: It's Shakespeare, Liz. And I'm directing it.
LIZZIE: Which makes it what?

RON: Real theatre.

LIZZIE: Do you hear yourself when you speak? This isn't a real theatre, this is a basement which is too dank to store food in and too dark to put anything worth seeing in. You're not a real director, you're just someone who's read a book of criticism one day earlier than everyone else and is the only one shameless enough to quote its words as your own. You're not a real artist, you're just a rich boy who could fly interstate or overseas to watch theatre that nobody else saw and you could steal wholesale and claim the ideas as your own. You're not a real person, your beard, your 'need to wear black during rehearsals' are all stolen affectations from actual people with actual interior lives. You're not real, you're a smirk covered in shitty cologne. Yes, I'm out of your show and yes I'm out of your life. See, got through that speech without the protection of an understudy—didn't I?

4.

The common room, later that night.

GILES *leans and holds up his phone to try and get the right angle so that he and his T-shirt can be in the shot. He gives up and just has a direct shot of the shirt and calls* GERT *on FaceTime.*

GERT: You're running for president. Great. Congrats.
GILES: That's all you've got to say?
GERT: Warren gave me the heads-up before you did.
GILES: You could be a bit more excited.
GERT: What am I meant to say in this situation?
GILES: Yay.
GERT: I'm not going to say 'yay'.
GILES: Can I get a 'Hip hop hooray'?
GERT: Are you going to win?
GILES: Warren thinks we can.
GERT: Is this your way of saying you're not coming?
GILES: If I win, my term would start at the end of the year. I can still visit.
GERT: So now you're just visiting huh?
GILES: What do you mean by that?
GERT: We discussed us staying on a bit longer. Travelling together. This adds a time limit to it all, no?

GILES: We didn't agree on that, did we?

GERT: We didn't agree on you running back scared after two weeks either.

GILES: What the fuck?

GERT: You're scared of leaving your safe little college cocoon so you do everything in your power to stay there.

GILES: How long have you been holding on to that?

GERT: Being in the real world has given me some perspective, is all.

GILES: You're on exchange, staying with your aunt in Islington. Cocoon calling the kettle black much?

GERT: I just think we're going in two different directions—you deciding on this presidency without discussing it is a perfect example of that.

GILES: What about you doing whatever it is you're doing in Europe. How's that for a different direction?

GERT: I can't have this conversation with you while you're drunk.

GILES: I'm not drunk. I'm just excited. I thought this would be a cool thing we could do. We talked about it at O-Week. You remember that, right?

GERT: We were kids when we said that.

GILES: We're still kids!

GERT: Don't ruin what we had by being snarky.

GILES: What's left to ruin?

GERT: I'll see you later, Gi.

GILES: Gert, I actually think we should really just finally—

> *The FaceTime ends. He's alone in the common room.*
>
> *A moment.*
>
> *He downloads an app on his phone, puts the phone down and goes and grabs a beer.*
>
> *The app sounds.*
>
> *He opens the beer.*
>
> *The app sounds again.*
>
> *He drinks the beer.*
>
> *He reads the message—the conversation is projected including the last two messages.*

BAAL2001: U up?
    ?!

GILES *sighs and starts typing.*

OPUSMAGNUM: ?
BAAL2001: Thought you'd disappeared on me.
OPUSMAGNUM: How's tings?
BAAL2001: Typo?
Drunk?

GILES *laughs.*

OPUSMAGNUM: Neither.
BAAL2001: Long time no text?
OPUSMAGNUM: Yeh. Busy.
BAAL2001: Everyone's busy. When someone says they're busy they mean they're 'important'.
OPUSMAGNUM: Judge not lest your glass house be stoned there fella.
BAAL2001: Oh the stoneable offences I have committed …
OPUSMAGNUM: I'd lift all bans if I was in charge of everything.
BAAL2001: If only …
OPUSMAGNUM: Could be happening sooner than you think.
BAAL2001: What you got bubbling?
OPUSMAGNUM: Something big.
BAAL2001: Big huh?
OPUSMAGNUM: Let's just say 'presidential'.
BAAL2001: From what I've seen you are totally presidential material.
OPUSMAGNUM: How so?
BAAL2001: When you stand to attention I can't help but salute.
OPUSMAGNUM: You're pure cheek.
BAAL2001: Maybe we should finally meet up. Can I come over?
OPUSMAGNUM: I'm going to sleep.
BAAL2001: So you wouldn't know if I came over.
OPUSMAGNUM: Why I got incognito. I'm invisible.
BAAL2001: You tease.
OPUSMAGNUM: Why?

BAAL2001 *sends a picture of their bare arse.*

BAAL2001: There's my pure cheek. Your turn to show me the 'something big you got bubbling'.

GILES *looks around and puts the camera down his pants and takes a photo.*

Blackout.

We hear the app noise again and again until it morphs into the birds of the morning.

5.

The next morning: the juice shop off campus.

TASH *stretches while sipping a juice.*

FIGARO *enters, in a puffer jacket, and sits beside her.*

FIGARO: When you said you wanted to meet at six I thought two things. One: who the fuck invented another six o'clock in the morning, two: this girl is a psycho.
TASH: Do I strike you as psycho?
FIGARO: Not worried about being seen with me out in the open?
TASH: It's six o'clock. At a juice bar. Unless you're worried about being recognised by tradies or yummie mummies. Besides, nobody on campus comes to this place.
FIGARO: I know one person.

    PRATCHETT *arrives.*

PRATCHETT: Dickhead.
FIGARO: Tory.
PRATCHETT: Dickhead.
TASH: Funny bumping into you here.
PRATCHETT: Bed was empty.
TASH: Babe, I promise I'm just just wrapping up.
PRATCHETT: You're always just—
TASH: Would you mind grabbing me a coffee?

    TASH *passes* PRATCHETT *a keep cup.*

FIGARO: Filter coffee of the day.

    FIGARO *reaches into his vest, finds and passes* PRATCHETT *a keep cup.*

    TASH *mouths 'love you'.* PRATCHETT *walks off.*

TASH: How you feeling? Pumped? First day of the election!
FIGARO: This isn't my first rodeo.

TASH: Then you'll know a thing or two about campaign T-shirts.

FIGARO: Human billboards. Great way to get the team colours out there.

TASH: What do you think of Giles's shirts?

FIGARO: Pretty standard.

TASH: What do you think of Giles's shirts?

FIGARO: … Pretty standard.

TASH: What do you think of Giles's shirts?

FIGARO: It says 'Giles' on it?

TASH: I've seen my share of campaign T-shirts in my day, you can expect typos, you can expect lettering that runs in the wash, but Giles's tees are the most immaculate examples I've ever seen. But that's just my opinion, what do you think of Giles's shirts?

FIGARO: I … oh. I'll get someone onto it.

TASH: Thanks for dropping by.

> PRATCHETT *puts a coffee down in front of* TASH *and gives* FIGARO *the keep cup full of suspicious yellow liquid.*

FIGARO: What's this?

PRATCHETT: It's Kenyan. It's new. You'll love it.

6.

A montage: every campaign stop appears in a social media video, picture or post (think Facebook, Instagram, TikTok) and is projected in the theatre in an ever-updating wall of content.

i.

The common room. WARREN *is there, stretching.*

The lounge room. PHILLIPA *is there, sipping from a sports bottle.*

The same blackboard exists in both rooms simultaneously.

It has two columns: one marked 'Giles', the other 'Lizzie'.

ii.

WARREN *writes 'Christians on Campus' on the blackboard.*

GILES *walks with a group of Christian students—holding the Bible, rosary beads, maybe there's a nun?*

ACT TWO

iii.

PHILLIPA *writes 'Arts Faculty'.*

LIZZIE *is in a book club—she stands up and reads from the book with verve and enthusiasm.*

iv.

Giles's campaign stall.

*It's busy, there's people signing up for things, there's campaign staff talking—*HANYA *is manning a table with T-shirts.* ANDY *enters.*

ANDY: Hey.

HANYA: Andy!

ANDY: I'd love a shirt, can I get a shirt?

HANYA: Of course.

ANDY: Can I get a large?

HANYA: Giles is really ready to step up funding for women's sports, dressing rooms and all.

ANDY: Sadly, the newspaper can't help candidates but I wanted to help out in person however I can.

    ANDY *picks up the sign-in sheet and fills it out.*

HANYA: I didn't know you knew Giles that well?

ANDY: I covered his rampage at the fencing tourno last year.

HANYA: 'Parry-noia!'

ANDY: That's right.

HANYA: We've been pumping it on socials. Who knew there were so many sabre heads out there?

ANDY: If that man can do to campus bureaucracy what he did to his opponents that day, he's got my vote.

    HANYA *checks the sheet.*

HANYA: You've ticked all the boxes—phone bank, human poster, door knocking—that's awesome. We've got a chalking session tonight, you're down for that?

ANDY: Literally whatever I need to say to get that shirt.

    HANYA *passes her a T-shirt from the box.*

HANYA: Thanks Andy—we'll be giving you a call.

ANDY: Pumped!
HANYA: Woo.
ANDY: Woo!

>HANYA *wanders off a bit weirded out.*

>ANDY *walks away from the stand and gives the shirt to* FIGARO.

FIGARO: Woo?

v.

WARREN *writes 'Islamic Students Association'.*

GILES *walks through with a group of Muslim students—maybe wearing a taqiyah hat, maybe a keffiyeh—he's in animated discussion.*

vi.

PHILLIPA *writes 'Science Faculty'.*

LIZZIE *wears a lab coat and looks through a microscope—she adjusts a dial then lets another student look through it, they fist pump and then jump up and down.*

vii.

A bike path on campus—after dark.

FIGARO *waits with the 'Giles!' T-shirt and anxiously checks his phone.*

A MAN *in a trench coat stands in the shadows behind him.*

MAN: Did you come alone?
FIGARO: Fuck me!
MAN: You would be so lucky.
FIGARO: You're the man who knows about the T-shirt.
MAN: Maybe, maybe not.

>*An awkward pause.*

FIGARO: Can you look at the shirt now or … ?
MAN: Pass it here.

>FIGARO *passes the* MAN *the shirt—he inspects it intricately.*

FIGARO: Well—
MAN: Exactly what I thought.
FIGARO: What?

MAN: This is one hundred percent cruelty-free fabric—it's a hemp and bamboo composite which is morally righteous but ludicrously expensive. Do you see the detail on the serifs?

FIGARO: No.

MAN: Of course not, you're not a specialist. The letter embossing alone would cost more than the one-thousand-dollar campaign spending limit. How many of these are there?

FIGARO: They've got boxes full.

MAN: Someone's being sneaky with accounting. They'll be recording all the units, that's easy to catch, but they will have put down the reduced price they scored rather than the market price which the anti-nepotism campaign finance rules demand.

FIGARO: How do you know?

MAN: Because that's what I do with every costume budget I've ever had.

FIGARO: How do we find out the market price of such a specific item?

MAN: Look at the tag, look up the website, find the price?

The MAN holds up the tag.

See? 'Chill Thrill Bill's Super Chill Shirt Emporium.Com'.

FIGARO: Oh. That was easy.

MAN: Anything to help Lizzie.

FIGARO: Oh, you know her?

MAN: I know she's been fucked around.

FIGARO: Oh really?

MAN: I've said all I can.

FIGARO takes the T-shirt back and leaves.

The MAN steps out of the shadow—it's STEW!

viii.

WARREN *writes 'Jewish Students Society'.*

GILES *is at a table with a group of Jewish students—he lights some candles, breaks some bread and cheers wine.*

ix.

PHILLIPA *writes 'business school'.*

LIZZIE *is in a mock-up of the Stock Exchange—she's wearing a vest. She yells with a bunch of other people holding pieces of paper in their hands.*

x.

MON *walks past with a sign saying 'Fill The Hole'.*

xi.

Everyone is reading the student newspaper—on their phones, in print copies.

HANYA *stands at the campaign table, folding T-shirts. She's hit with a spotlight, she puts her arms up and perp walks to the front of the stage.*

HANYA: Although I feel I have done nothing wrong, I feel it is in the best interest for myself and for the campaign for me to step down immediately from any and all roles within the Giles movement. Please consider this the end of the matter.

The world moves on from HANYA.

xii.

A bar.

TASH *sits on a lounge with* PRATCHETT. *They make out.*

FIGARO *arrives.*

FIGARO *clears his throat.*

They stop making out. TASH *checks her make-up.*

PRATCHETT: Dickhead.
FIGARO: Failed novelist.
PRATCHETT: How did you know?
FIGARO: I didn't but I'm now going to make it my life's mission to find that Google Doc.
PRATCHETT: Should never have welcomed this vampire into our house.
TASH: Can I get another vodka sunrise minus the sunrise, love?
PRATCHETT: You're not meant to be drinking while you're thesis writing.
TASH: Can I get a sunrise then?
FIGARO: Pespi Max?

    PRATCHETT *leaves.*

How's the thesis?

TASH: I don't know what it is about ancient civilisations that is so fascinating. Probably cause it seems like they figured it out and we're just fucking it up. Must be why kids like dinosaurs on some subliminal level.

    FIGARO *yawns.*

I'm boring you?
FIGARO: A little.
TASH: At least you're honest. It's driving Pratchett up the bloody walls. She's graduated, she couldn't care less about theses or elections, she just wants her girlfriend back. How's the newspaper business?
FIGARO: After the Hanya exposé, a law firm asked for a few full-page ads today and there's talk of the Defence Force throwing some cash towards a 'We Want You' style recruitment campaign as a permanent back page, so I'm happy with our arrangements.
TASH: A rising tide helps all ships.
FIGARO: It drowned Hanya.
TASH: She'll survive.
FIGARO: You got anymore info or am I just here to watch you and your girlfriend bicker?
TASH: What do you know about Kev?
FIGARO: Sprang from the earth fully formed.
TASH: Kev's quite a big guy.
FIGARO: Why we had the Brisbane line I suppose.
TASH: I said Kev's quite a big guy.
FIGARO: Oh.

    PRATCHETT *returns with a shot of vodka for* TASH *and a glass of suspicious yellow liquid for* FIGARO.

FIGARO: What's this?
PRATCHETT: It's Pepsi. New colouring. You'll love it.

xiii.

PHILLIPA *writes 'social justice alliance'.*

LIZZIE *walks through with a protest sign in hand, by herself, chanting.*

xiv.

WARREN *writes 'Sports' on the board'.*

GILES *runs across the stage holding a rugby ball, he is pursued by a rugby team.*

xv.

The 'I'm With Lizzie!' campaign stall.

KEV *plays on his phone.*

ELISE: 'Do you even squat?'
KEV: What the fuck you say?
ELISE: 'Do you even want a Kim K butt?'
KEV: Elise. Mate, I'm too busy with this campaign stuff to do a profile right now.
ELISE: Mate. I'm not here for a profile. I'm here to join the campaign.
KEV: Right on. Not a conflict of interest with the paper?
ELISE: Job can't tell me how I can and can't vote.
KEV: Tell that to south-west Queensland.
ELISE: Where do you work out?
KEV: Odd question, no segue, seems fair.
ELISE: You're looking pretty massive these days.
KEV: You looking at getting back on the iron horse?
ELISE: My gym sucks. Its title reminds me that I could be working out literally *anytime* and I don't like the judgement you know?
KEV: I work out at Beefhead's, do you know it?
ELISE: Thought it was a steak restaurant?
KEV: It is on top of the Ala-moo Tex-Mex Steakhouse and below Gentleman Beef's Meat Emporium so I can see why you'd think that. Tell Sally Kev sent you and you'll get a sweet discount.
ELISE: Cheers bro.

They shake hands, KEV *accidentally crushes* ELISE*'s hand.*

xvi.

PHILLIPA *writes 'Expressions of Culture'.*

LIZZIE *lights candles for a Hindu cultural festival.*

xvii.

GILES *runs back across bouncing a basketball, he is pursued by a basketball team.*

xviii.

Beefhead's Gym.

It's not fancy—think lumberjacks doing CrossFit. SALLY *walks in with* FIGARO.

SALLY: That's the set-up.
FIGARO: Where's the cardio?

    SALLY *laughs.*

So have you got a trial program? One week free sort of thing?
SALLY: We take cash on the door. You pay, you play. You don't, you won't.
FIGARO: I'm not sure if it's right for me though.
SALLY: If you're thinking that then it's definitely not.
FIGARO: How do I get as big as Kev?
SALLY: Genetics. You've seen his brothers?
FIGARO: I have.
SALLY: Because you're friends.
FIGARO: Real close.
SALLY: You don't look like his regular friends.
FIGARO: That's why he sent me here.
SALLY: He's a good man. Great heart on him, always wants others to do better.
FIGARO: Real sweetheart.
SALLY: Well he won't mind me saying, but when he came in here, he was about your size.
FIGARO: No?
SALLY: True, we got him on a meat diet downstairs, got him throwing the kettlebells, a little bit of—

    SALLY *whistles.*

And here he is.

    FIGARO *whistles.*

    SALLY *nods and whistles.*

FIGARO: Where would I get the—

    FIGARO *whistles while he grabs his wallet and hands her a wad of cash.*

    SALLY *looks around, reaches behind her and pulls out an esky.*
    FIGARO *opens it.*

SALLY: Before that, I've gotta get you on the chin-ups.

> FIGARO *is taken to a chin-up bar. He does not do well, to say the least.*

xix.

PHILLIPA *writes 'Other Interests'.*

LIZZIE *balances books on her head poorly. They fall—she walks off.*

xx.

GILES *runs back across holding a fencing foil. He is pursued by a man in fencing gear.*

GILES *collapses.*

xxi.

Everyone reads the student newspaper—on their phones, in print copies.

KEV *does push-ups, a spotlight hits him, he stands up—sweaty, sad. He perp-walks towards the front of the stage.*

KEV: I am not a perfect man and I have never claimed to be. It is due to the amount of respect I hold for the candidate and for the campaign that effectively immediately I am no longer associated in any form, corporeal or financial, with the I'm with Lizzie! Campaign. Please respect my privacy during this trying time.

> *The world moves on from* KEV. HANYA *approaches him with a cup of coffee.*

xxii.

An Italian restaurant.

White tablecloths, roses in a vase, candles lit.

PRATCHETT: Tash, baby. This has been the greatest few years of my life.

TASH: Oh my god, oh my god.

> PRATCHETT *kneels down on one knee and gets out a box.*
>
> FIGARO *walks in and waves.*

PRATCHETT: No.

TASH: Sorry baby.

PRATCHETT: Could it wait like two minutes?

TASH: You're so cuuuuuute. Could you get me another glass of rosé?

FIGARO: I'm pretty sure the last two times, you've given me a glass of piss. Can I get *not* that?

> PRATCHETT *stands up and walks away.*

Sorry about the interruption.

TASH: This is like the sixth time she's proposed. We cool.

FIGARO: You saw Kev.

TASH: Poor Kev.

FIGARO: Poor dumb Kev.

TASH: Poor dumb beautiful Kev.

FIGARO: Beautiful?

TASH: I've got a type. Malleability and strength should not be overestimated in a political spouse.

FIGARO: I'm never getting married.

TASH: That won't be up to you. Newspaper going well? I see people reading the paper a lot more than they used to.

FIGARO: People love watching things collapse.

TASH: Speaking of things rising and falling, in my time as president I got to know a number of the more colourful members of the campus community. One of which gave me a divine insight into the student body and how they are uniquely gifted with two abilities. One: they will give away absolutely anything for free wi-fi, and two: they will use that free wi-fi to send pictures of their nudes and lewds across campus.

FIGARO: Here we go.

TASH: There's a dick pic.

FIGARO: Now that's a fucking segue. Okay, and how do I find it?

TASH: Zoom, of course.

xxiii.

PHILLIPA *writes 'Creative Arts Collective' on the board.*

LIZZIE *does an incredibly precise and perfect mime routine—it is sad as it is beautiful. A crowd erupts in cheers.*

LIZZIE *collapses in a chair next to* PHILLIPA.

xxvii.

FIGARO *in a Zoom meeting room.*

FIGARO *waits.*

He picks his nose.

SPARROW *appears, wearing a medieval plague doctor's mask and with his voice distorted.*

SPARROW: Figaro Lozarno I presume.
FIGARO: How did you know my name?
SPARROW: It's at the bottom of your screen.
FIGARO: Right.

> SPARROW *takes off his mask, he's your standard IT guy.*

SPARROW: Sorry I was coming from a LARP convention. I hear on the wind you are after a picture of a penis.
FIGARO: And I've heard you're the person to see on campus about finding said picture of a penis.
SPARROW: You have no idea how many dicks I see a day.
FIGARO: … thousands?
SPARROW: None.
FIGARO: I don't understand.
SPARROW: I see the trail of the penis, not the actual tip. Or balls.
FIGARO: You see the envelope. Not the letter.
SPARROW: Do you know who sent the envelope?
FIGARO: No.
SPARROW: Do you know who wrote the letter?
FIGARO: No.
SPARROW: But you know there's a dick in the envelope.
FIGARO: I know it could rock the whole election.
SPARROW: Which means it's one of three people.
FIGARO: And as far as i'm aware, only one of them has the required equipment.
SPARROW: Suit yourself. Have you got the man's campus address?

> FIGARO *sends an address through text.*

Now, all we have to do is narrow
   The
   Parameters

Of
Our
Search
To
This
Address
And ...
BAM!
There's your dick!
There's your envelope!
And that's where it went!
Tell Tash, we're even.

SPARROW *leaves the Zoom room.*

7.

Close to midnight.

The lounge room of the sharehouse.

The common room of the college.

GILES *and* LIZZIE *are in various stages of exhaustion—maybe they nurse a tea or beer, they're definitely covered in blankets, it's been a big three weeks.*

PHILLIPA *and* WARREN *scroll madly through their phones, trying to digest and be across a large amount of information until ...*

PHILLIPA/WARREN: Okay ...
LIZZIE: Have you seen Kev since ... ?
GILES: I haven't seen Hanya for a bit.
PHILLIPA: Either doing push-ups or at the pub.
WARREN: Probably shopping or something.
LIZZIE: I feel bad.
GILES: She was only trying to help.
WARREN: She'll be fine.
PHILLIPA: He'll land on his feet. Now it's been a big few weeks.
WARREN: Massive few weeks.
LIZZIE: I know.
GILES: I was there.

PHILLIPA: We're getting responses trickling back in.
WARREN: We've got polls out in the field and their results are back.
GILES/LIZZIE: And?
PHILLIPA: We asked people.
WARREN: We texted people.
PHILLIPA: And they were quite frank in their reply.
WARREN: And they texted back.
GILES/LIZZIE: So … ?!
GILES: Are we fucked?
LIZZIE: How'd we go?

> WARREN *and* PHILLIPA *write out '80%' and '60%' respectively.*

WARREN: We needed eighty percent of those groups approached.
PHILLIPA: We needed sixty percent of those groups approached.
WARREN: Your early visits to the religious groups did phenomenally well.

> WARREN *ticks 'Christians on Campus', 'Islamic Students Association', 'Jewish Students Society'.*

PHILLIPA: The faculties associations loved you.

> PHILLIPA *ticks 'Arts Faculty', 'Science Faculty', 'Business School'.*

WARREN: The middle week dedicated to the colleges
GILES: Lost me a lot of brain cells.
WARREN: Gained you a lot of votes.
GILES: Lost me a lot of brain cells. Did I say that already?

> WARREN *ticks 'Sports'.*

WARREN: We expected that the T-shirt scandal would cut us, but thought Hanya's apology and withdrawal would staunch more bleeding than it did.

> WARREN *crosses out some of the voting blocs.*

PHILLIPA: Kev's 'roid usage got us a lot of rage.
LIZZIE: Did you know he was using?
PHILLIPA: His mood swings make a lot more sense now.

> PHILLIPA *crosses out some of the voting blocs.*

Your mime, god knows why, worked. Creative arts rallied behind you—you're one of their own, you obviously care and they even agreed that Kevin did the right thing so …

> PHILLIPA *does a big tick next to 'creative arts collective'.*

GILES: My brain's not working.
LIZZIE: Where does this leave us?

> PHILLIPA *and* WARREN *do a quick maths on the board.*
>
> *They ultimately cross out the '80%' and '60%'.*
>
> PHILLIPA *writes down '55.55%'.*
>
> WARREN *writes down '66.6%'.*

PHILLIPA: We need sixty percent, we got fifty-five-point-five percent.
WARREN: We need eighty percent, we got sixty-six-point-six percent.
PHILLIPA: We're pretty certain that the support we've lost,
WARREN: We're not going to get back.
PHILLIPA: But we're not the only ones who lost support this cycle,
WARREN: There's still some votes to get on the other side. We're going to reach beyond the base.
PHILLIPA: We're going into the belly of the beast.
GILES/LIZZIE: How?
PHILLIPA: The good news is this election is attracting a lot of attention.
WARREN: The bad news is this election is attracting a lot of attention.
PHILLIPA/WARREN: So it's all going to come down to
GILES/LIZZIE: The debate.

8.

The student theatre.

RON *steps through a swordfight by himself in the space whilst reciting ...*

RON: Romans, countrymen, and lovers! Hear me for my cause, and be silent, that you may hear; believe me for mine honour, and have respect to mine honour, that you may believe; censure me in your wisdom, and awake your senses, that you may the better judge.

> FIGARO *claps and enters.*

Aha—thank you kind soul. Just a little warm-up, we had an actor pull out. I've got auditions tomorrow but just in case I need to step on.
FIGARO: Ably so.
RON: You are?

FIGARO: Figaro.
RON: The chief servant of the house.
FIGARO: Journalist.
RON: Opera.
FIGARO: Dad tried to get me to listen to it but it went—

> FIGARO *whooshes over his head.*

RON: Why's your name so familiar to me?
FIGARO: I'm a bit of a BNOC.
RON: You wrote the brutal review of the dance theatre piece Lizzie directed outside. What was the headline?
FIGARO: 'Mao's Worst Cancer.'
RON: Ha!
FIGARO: Don't hold that against me.
RON: Between me, you and the ghosts of this theatre? I agreed with you.
FIGARO: That's good to hear. I can't say I've actually ever stepped foot in here.
RON: Different points of view about the value of this place. Some want to throw shit on the walls and see what sticks before they head off to be accountants or lawyers or umbrella salespeople.
FIGARO: Others want to create art that explores what it means to be human and push emotions to the extreme in an attempt to galvanise and terrify.
RON: You saw my production of *Baal*?
FIGARO: Bertolt Brecht's juvenile ode to a poet that society couldn't control. No, I didn't watch, but I relate.
RON: You're quoting my director's notes?
FIGARO: Not many people like that play.
RON: Because not many people understand that play.
FIGARO: You're writing your thesis on it?
RON: The theatre of the wunderkind.
FIGARO: Is that what you are doing down here in this theatre?
RON: That's up for others to decide.
FIGARO: You're what? Twenty-one?
RON: So still in the age bracket? Again, if others decide I'm that, so be it.

FIGARO: Means you were born in (two thousand and one).
RON: So …
FIGARO: Baal2001 is a perfect username for you then.

> *Pause.*

> When you put it together like that, it sounds pretty brazen.

RON: So you found my profile on a dating app, so what? Did we match?
FIGARO: You've got a girlfriend.
RON: Monogamy's a medieval concept. I'm not ashamed.
FIGARO: I'm not saying you should be. Journalism isn't about shaming, you can do whatever you want, with whoever you want, I'm not stopping you.
RON: Then why do you come to me late at night with such foreboding?
FIGARO: There's an ongoing contest, upstairs in the real world, between privacy and the public interest. A presidential candidate's boyfriend having a secret epistolic affair with another candidate feels like it fits that remit.

> *Pause.*

> I know he sent you a photo. Must've felt good to get that picture from someone like him. Made you feel powerful, probably? Connected, definitely. I just wanted to drop by and say that I'll be bringing it up at the debate so you might want to give your girlfriend a call.

RON: Ex.
FIGARO: Sorry?
RON: Ex-girlfriend. Lizzie and I are done.
FIGARO: Interesting. Do you want to get her back?
RON: Of course I do.
FIGARO: I was going to just throw you under the bus but maybe there's a more mutually agreeable point? I scratch your back, you stab hers? I'm sure you of all people will have no problem considering such human emotions being pushed to the extreme.
RON: What are you proposing?
FIGARO: I thought the idea of the photo was damaging enough. But, the image itself?
RON: What?
FIGARO: I have no idea.
RON: Will it win her back?

FIGARO: If used properly.

    FIGARO leaves and RON sits on the ground.

RON: For Brutus, as you know, was Caesar's angel. Judge, O you gods, how dearly Ceasar loved him! This was the most most unkindest of cuts.

    He pulls the rope and is covered in the bucket of blood.

9.

Night.

Underneath a street light, MON keeps warm by marching back and forth with her sign saying 'Fill the hole!'

She is approached from a distance by two figures.

They get closer and closer, but only one steps under the street light.

HANYA: You're Mon, right?

    MON nods.

We'd like to help out on your mission.

    Another person steps into the light.

KEV: Yeah, we've got a few ideas of who you could put in that hole.
HANYA: Ready for the campaign to start?
MON: I've been campaigning for the last few weeks.
KEV: Tomorrow, the real campaign begins.
MON: What do you mean?
HANYA: Banners, posters, pamphlets—it's quite the spectacle.
KEV: What do you reckon? I think if she stood up straighter.
HANYA: I know a jacket that would rock with her hair.
MON: Who are you?
HANYA: Us?
KEV: We're your new campaign team.

                    INTERVAL

ACT THREE: THE DEBATE

1.

The bare stage at the university bar.

The debate is being set up: three lecterns are wheeled on, a table with chairs is set up over the following.

Once set up, ANDY *sits behind the moderators' table.*

ANDY: Could we test number one?

    WARREN *and* GILES, *wearing a bright pink shirt and dungarees.* GILES *goes through palm cards in his hand.*

GILES: It's too much.
ANDY: Hey Warren!

    WARREN *holds up his hand.*

WARREN: Warren.
ANDY: Still doing that huh? Just trying out levels. Could you—

    Mic is turned on.

GILES: Hello. Hello. Hello.
ANDY: We're getting a bit of an echo.

    Beat. GILES *is unsure whether he's joking. The mic's turned off.*

WARREN: The point is it *is* too much. That's what kids love these days.
GILES: Dressing like the Rugrats?
WARREN: Exactly. You could mumble a bit more.
GILES: Mumble?
WARREN: Like the rappers. You over-articulate.
GILES: There are articulate rappers.

    Mic is back on.

ANDY: We think we've worked it out.

    GILES *is a bit more mumbley than before.*

GILES: My money don't jiggle, jiggle, it folds.
　　I like to see you wiggle, wiggle, for sure.
ANDY: It makes me wanna dribble, dribble, you know.

The mic's turned off.

WARREN *pulls out a glasses case.*

WARREN: Now, feel free to say no.
GILES: No.
WARREN: Just try them and see how they feel.
GILES: No.

GILES *puts down his palm cards to take the glasses and they walk off.*

ANDY: Any word on Monica? Has anyone seen Monica?!

LIZZIE *comes on, wearing a blazer and glasses.* PHILLIPA *follows.*

　Hey Lizzie.
PHILLIPA: Hey Andy.
ANDY: P, we're just running levels.

LIZZIE *leans into the microphone.*

LIZZIE: She sells sea shells by the sea shore.
ANDY: Can we get rid of that hiss? Sorry Lizzie, bear with us.

The mic's turned off.

LIZZIE: Does the blazer look good? I got it off my mum.
PHILLIPA: You look a bit like an ad exec.
LIZZIE: That's the point. Corporate can't hurt.
PHILLIPA: Never thought I'd hear you say that.
LIZZIE: You said we needed to expand our votes.
PHILLIPA: I'm not sure changing clothes is going to give us an edge.

The mic's turned back on.

ANDY: I didn't know you wore glasses.
LIZZIE: For reading. Sometimes.
ANDY: They look good. Very
PHILLIPA: Corporate?
ANDY: Serious. Like you're taking this seriously.
LIZZIE: I am,

ACT THREE

PHILLIPA: Finally.
ANDY: That's great for levels.
LIZZIE: Would you mind calling me Elizabeth? Not Lizzie? But Elizabeth?
ANDY: Of course. Thanks guys—see you in a minute.

The mic's turned off.

PHILLIPA: Are they even real lenses?
LIZZIE: I got them from the prop room.

PHILLIPA and LIZZIE turn to leave.

LIZZIE notices GILES's palm cards and picks them up.

PHILLIPA: What's that?
LIZZIE: Our edge.

They leave.

ELISE enters, ANDY stands up.

ANDY: All set up, homie. You're good to go.

FIGARO enters behind her.

ELISE: Please for the love of god, leave me alone or I will crucify you. I know that's a saying, I will actually crucify you. I did woodwork in high school and I'm pretty sure that every single bit of fitting and joinery that is in the back of my brain would flood back if I gave it a chance and opened up these gates of rage.

ANDY turns off the microphone.

ANDY: Let me turn off the microphone before you threaten murder.
FIGARO: Hear me out.
ELISE: I have been hearing you out, the entire walk here. And last night when I was trying to sleep. And the night before when I was visiting my aunt in hospital.
FIGARO: She better?
ELISE: Well, it's honestly a bit touch and go so—
FIGARO: Andy, I want to do the panel.
ANDY: But this is a university event?
FIGARO: I'm aware.
ANDY: Elise does events.
FIGARO: It's a political matter, I'm the political reporter, this is my domain.
ELISE: You made that decision yourself.

FIGARO: Are we a hard-hitting newspaper or are we a gig guide with a crossword?

> *Beat.*

ANDY/ELISE: Gig guide with a crossword.
ELISE: Sorry little man, that's two editors versus one.

> ELISE *sits down at the table and opens up her folder and points something out to* ANDY *to draw their attention away from* FIGARO.

I say if we can cut off their mics, we should do it, how do I do that from here Andy?
ANDY: You've done good, mate. People from ESPN have been looking at my LinkedIn page. Super cool huh?
FIGARO: Super duper cool.
ANDY: They wouldn't have seen my articles without your coverage so thanks man. Elise does events, rules are rules.

> ANDY *leans over the desk and starts fiddling with the cords.*

ELISE: Sadly, you don't get to swan in, cover a few scandals—
FIGARO: Uncover, thank you.
ELISE: Sure, *uncover* two scandals.
FIGARO: Three.
ELISE: Nobody cares.
FIGARO: I uncovered *three* scandals.
ELISE: It's not what we're about.
FIGARO: It seems to be what the *Guardian* is about.
ANDY: Why do you keep saying three?
FIGARO: It seems to be what *The Australian* is about.
ANDY: You didn't uncover three scandals, Figaro.

> FIGARO *holds up one finger.*

Hanya's T-shirts.
ELISE: Andy?

> FIGARO *holds up two fingers.*

ANDY: Kev's drugs.
ELISE: Andy!

> FIGARO *holds up three fingers.*

ANDY: What's the third?

FIGARO *shrugs.*

He knows something. What do you know?

FIGARO: Exclusive, mate. I'll probably just take it elsewhere, get a sick internship. I mean if I kept the scoop here, you would reap the rewards. Imagine working at ESPN instead of just lurking in their YouTube comments section hoping someone notices.

ANDY: Don't fuck with me.

FIGARO: Would I do that?

ELISE: Yes. Yes he would.

ANDY: I will gut you if this is a lie.

FIGARO: Put your fishing knife away.

Beat. ANDY *closes* ELISE*'s folder.*

That's two editors versus one.

ELISE: Don't do this. You'll regret this. He's going to do the same to you Andy, I'm the only thing standing between you and a knife in the back.

ANDY: Probably. Sorry mate. You'd do the same. It's not personal.

ELISE: I wouldn't.

ANDY: It's journalism. You understand?

ELISE *gets up and picks up her folder.*

ELISE: Student. You meant to say 'It's not personal, it's *student* journalism'. Have a little fucking perspective.

FIGARO *sits down, looks up at* ELISE *and shrugs.*

FIGARO: Grab a beer Elise, you're gonna wanna watch this one.

The lights start to dip on the debate stage.

2.

The stage looks different under these lights: more professional somehow.

The university emblem is projected onto the back of the stage—maybe it spins?

FIGARO: Welcome to the (twenty-twenty-two) Student Council Presidential Debate.

He encourages applause.

Tonight's debate marks a chance for last minute introductions, audience interaction, hard questions and final statements.

He's distracted for a moment.

And yes, the venue manager is reminding me that once the debate is over please leave in an orderly fashion because some grown men have reserved the space afterwards so that they can play Nintendo and drink beer on the big screen. Ah the contrasts you only get at university. Alright, without much further ado, your candidates. Please give a welcome round of applause for Giles O'Hagan.

GILES *enters: pink shirt, dungarees, and now a pair of polarised glasses.*

He stands behind his platform and over the following, looks for his palm cards.

Elizabeth 'Lizzie' Somers.

LIZZIE *enters: sensible blazer and reading glasses and stands behind a lectern.*

Monica DePuissant.

The lights go off.

Monica DePuissant?

'Break the Rules' by Charli XCX plays.

Monica?

MON *enters: white pant-suit, still has a moon boot, but extremely confident.*

The chorus ends, the song stops and the lights return to normal.

Well that was ... wow. Our intern [insert Celebrity Cameo] has been busy gathering voter data over the last little while. What have you got for us tonight?

Cutaway to CELEBRITY CAMEO, *who reads out the results from the poll taken at intermission.*

CELEBRITY CAMEO: Thanks for having me. This opportunity is really going to look good on the resume. The current pre-polling results see [Z] in third place on [percentage], [Y] in second on [percentage] and [X] at first, steaming ahead on [percentage].

ACT THREE

FIGARO: Fascinating, fascinating. Still a week to go. Fascinating. Great work, I'll be sure to write you a glowing reference. Right then, let's get into the debate. To decide the speaking order, we're going to do an old-fashioned coin toss and since we don't have a three-sided coin, we're going to do elimination. Lizzie?

LIZZIE: Heads.

GILES: Tails.

MON taps her butt.

FIGARO: Okay then.

FIGARO flips the coin.

Heads it is. Lizzie. Sorry, Elizabeth. You'll go first. You've got one minute.

A red digital timer appears behind them.

LIZZIE: Thank you Figaro, thank you everyone for being here today. You know this university has meant a lot to me over the years. When I was in high school I looked to it as a beacon on the hill. To walk through its hallowed halls would be an achievement of a lifetime. Now that I'm here, it has taken up an even larger place in my life than I could ever have expected. Yes, a place of learning but also a home and the mana that animates this place is its student council. As president, I don't just want to ensure that it's kept that way for those who follow me, I want to make it better, make it more available, and make it more diverse.

LIZZIE looks at PHILLIPA. PHILLIPA shakes her head. LIZZIE takes out the palm cards.

That's not without saying that this place isn't built on a strong platform. For too long the role of the colleges has been dismissed, the role of religion pushed to the side and the proud sporting achievements of this institution minimised. I want the people in those halls to know that my name is Elizabeth Somers and I stand for you.

FIGARO: Giles.

The clock resets. GILES *is still stunned from* LIZZIE*'s speech.*

Giles.

WARREN: Oi!

> GILES *shakes out of it and* WARREN *starts madly writing something down on a piece of paper.*

GILES: Hi.

> *Beat.*

I'm Giles. O'Hagan. Giles O'Hagan. And I'm running for president of the student council.

> *Beat.*

Hi. I'm—

> LIZZIE *smiles and waves back holding his palm cards.*

Lizzie!

LIZZIE: No, you're Giles.

GILES: Yes. I'm Giles.

> *Beat.*

I am a college student, I am a religious student and I play sport.

> *Beat.*

For too long the role of the colleges has been dismissed, the role of religion pushed to the side and the proud sporting achievements of this institution minimised. I want the people in those halls to know that my name is Giles O'Hagan and I—

> FIGARO *rings a bell.*

FIGARO: Sorry, time's up. Monica?

> WARREN *comes on and passes the new speech to* GILES.

WARREN: [*to* GILES] Snap out of it, okay?

MON: Fellow students.

WARREN: Sorry, sorry, he's got low blood sugar.

> WARREN *leaves.*

MON: I am not a politician.
    I am not one of them.
    I am one of you.
    I do not want a lot.
    In fact, I want just one thing.

ACT THREE

One thing that has been left broken for too long.
With your help ...
I can do it.
With your help,
We can do it.
Together, we could ...
Together, we should ...
Together, we will ...
Fill.
The.
Hole!

The timer hits zero.

MON *steps back.*

FIGARO: The president of the student council has a mandate so broad it would make the most experienced executive in the public and private sphere blush. How does your experience position you to undertake this? Giles.

GILES *unfolds the script.*

GILES: Thank you Figaro and sorry for the little brain-fart before, seems I've misplaced my cue cards. But now that I've lowered the bar sufficiently and we're on the topic of money I think I can speak with a bit more authority. The financial viability and sustainability of this organisation is at the heart of my campaign. Yes, everything is working and we're stronger than ever but if COVID has taught us anything—strength is a moment away from weakness. I'm comfortable enough to realise what my weaknesses are, where my strengths are, and there's a lot of people who are a lot more comfortable with spending money than me. My weakness is—yes, my instinct is to be stingy—because the clubs and departments have sucked on the teet of our fair organisation, and my job above all will be to ensure the survivability of this organisation, and I'm not above cutting off the runt from the teat.

GILES *turns to* WARREN *and mouths 'Runt from the teat?'*

LIZZIE *claps and laughs.*

I'm glad you find financial common sense such a funny topic. Glad but not surprised.

LIZZIE: I'm laughing at your hypocrisy. And the reference to teats.

GILES: How am I being hypocritical?

FIGARO: You are talking about the exposé our newspaper did on Hanya?

LIZZIE: I am, yes.

FIGARO: For those who are not following this as closely as us political junkies, the second in command of Giles's campaign had spent fifteen times the spending cap on T-shirts.

GILES: And she has resigned.

FIGARO: But the point still stands: how can you be trusted with the keys to a thirty-million-dollar organisation when you can't be trusted to handle a one-thousand-dollar spending cap?

LIZZIE: I'd like a crack at that Figaro.

GILES: The question was directed at me.

FIGARO: Elizabeth, you can go first, then Giles, you can respond.

LIZZIE: Thank you. You asked Giles or Lil' G or whoever he'll be dressed up as tomorrow how can he be trusted with the keys to a thirty-million-dollar organisation when he can't be trusted to handle a one-thousand-dollar spending cap? It's easy. He's proven he can't be trusted with either.

GILES: Hanya had very good intentions.

    WARREN *does a stabbing motion.*

But I've taken her rank abuse of funds as a great personal betrayal. She has been let go, we have not communicated since, and I don't see that happening again in the future. As far as I am concerned, the matter is closed.

FIGARO: Monica, do you have anything to add?

    Beat.

Mon?

    Beat.

Monica DePuissant?
Do you have anything to add?

    MON *leans forward.*

MON: Nothing except … Fill the hole. Thank you.

    MON *leans back.*

ACT THREE

FIGARO: Okay, moving on. As the leader of a peak advocacy group representing over thirty thousand students on this campus and satellite campuses around the city, what do you think makes you stand above the other candidates? Monica, your turn to go first.

MON: Thank you.

I'm not going to spout about achievements or accolades. We're all on the same stage, we're all equally qualified.

There is a hole located exactly where the bus from town lets you off.

Is it a large hole? No.

Is it a small hole? Who can say?

Is it an inconvenient hole? Definitely.

So why has it gone unnoticed for all this time?

Because it sits out the front of a bus stop that sits outside the traditional remit of the two traditional candidates you see before you.

GILES: Come on.

FIGARO: Giles, no interruptions. Monica, please start your point again.

MON: I'll be fine, thank you. The man over there made my real point for me. Our voices are unimportant, our concerns are not valid and our inconveniences are trivial to them.

MON indicates GILES and LIZZIE.

Lucky I'm not one of them. I'm one of you, and together we're gonna fill that hole. Thank you.

MON steps back.

FIGARO: Elizabeth?

LIZZIE: I could talk about how I was part of an acclaimed outdoor one-woman version of *Mao's Last Dancer* for the student theatre society. I could talk about how I organised the largest conga line in human history to raise awareness for period stigma right here on campus. But instead I want to take the clock back a few years to a French lecture just down the road. I want you to imagine a young girl in a denim jacket and floral dress who was convinced she was going to be a diplomat, and the only way to do that was to become fluent in French. She didn't know where she was going, what she was doing, or who she was. She took a seat somewhere in the middle and she sat on a flier. That flier was an introduction event run by the student university council and that girl? That girl was me.

Pause for applause.

Over the past few years at university I have held a variety of positions across a number of clubs and societies—you can find them on my website I'mWithLizzie.com—the things I've learned along the way are clear and can be counted on less than one hand. Surround yourself with the best people. Actively listen. Learn. I will carry that through to this role. Thank you.

FIGARO: I'd like to pick up on a point of yours. Surrounding yourself with the best people …

LIZZIE: I know where this is going and I'd like to intercept it.

FIGARO: I didn't get to my question.

LIZZIE: You're unfairly bringing up Kev.

GILES: What's unfair about it?

LIZZIE: He stepped down.

GILES: So did Hanya.

LIZZIE: Hanya committed mass financial fraud.

GILES: Kev was using a veterinary-grade pharmaceutical.

LIZZIE: You've never done the same?

> GILES *turns to* FIGARO *for him to interject, but he doesn't.*

FIGARO: It's up to you whether you answer this or not, Giles.

LIZZIE: Have you done drugs?

> WARREN *from the sidelines does a spinning motion with his finger.*

GILES: Would that not be my choice?

> WARREN *fist bumps the air.*

LIZZIE: Answer the question.

> WARREN *does a stabbing motion.*

GILES: Would that not be a matter of bodily autonomy?

LIZZIE: Really—you're going to spin it like that?

GILES: Stigma, ladies and gentleman. She is stigmatising me!

LIZZIE: You're making this about—

GILES: Choice? I thought that was something you cared about. I thought that's what *democracy* was all about.

LIZZIE: That's not what I mean.

ACT THREE 69

GILES: You keep saying what you don't mean, what do you mean?

LIZZIE: You make a deal of it being bad that someone on my campaign was found with drugs, but you refuse to answer whether you do drugs. When your college has been swamped with allegations of rampant cocaine usage.

GILES: There you go again, attacking the colleges you seek to represent.

LIZZIE: I think there's an element of hypocrisy in your current stance that could do with some sunlight. Or bleach. Or fire.

GILES: Is it a question of judgement? In your experience, how much judgement does it take to smoke as much weed as you do?

LIZZIE: About the same as getting blackout drunk.

GILES: There you go again, attacking colleges.

LIZZIE: I didn't say colleges.

GILES: The use of 'blackout drunk' has long-term negative—

LIZZIE: Fine, I am attacking colleges.

GILES: Thank you.

LIZZIE: Not the people who live there.

GILES: What? Do you hate sandstone?

LIZZIE: I hate systems of oppression that you not only take part in but that you benefit from and that you perpetuate.

GILES: Is my very existence triggering to you?

LIZZIE: I imagine I'm not the only one.

FIGARO: Monica?

> MON *steps forward.*
>
> *She smiles.*
>
> *She stares straight ahead.*
>
> *She fiddles with her papers.*
>
> *She looks out at the crowd.*
>
> *She folds her arms.*
>
> *She adjusts her belt.*

MON: Fill the hole.

FIGARO: We're opening up to the audience.

> *Audience question one is for* GILES—*no matter what it is, the answer below follows:*

GILES: It is actually the most important job, the most important job that the student council has in managing its funds, to get its members into the activities that look good on a resume and read well in a memoir, to ensure that after university they get the jobs, the jobs, the jobs. But when you have never done a budget, you have no idea about the implications of what you're saying for other ways of how it impacts on the budget. If she's that precious, and she can't hack a campaign, then how on earth is she going to handle running this council?

Question two: for MON—*clears her throat.*

MON: Each day, the hole grows larger. Each day, the hole swallows more of us. Each day, they build their tower higher and higher. But one day, it will swallow us all. Unless we fill the hole. Thank you.

MON *steps back.*

RON *emerges from the audience—more dishevelled than before, he's drunk on red wine and is still covered in the blood from before.*

RON: I have a question about arts policy.
LIZZIE: Go home Ron.
GILES: Nobody cares about the arts.
FIGARO: No, no, a question's a question.
RON: Given the devastating effects that COVID has had and continues to have on the arts sector, will you raise or cut funding for the theatre?
FIGARO: Lizzie?
LIZZIE: I may not believe in your art, Ron but I will fight to the death for it to be moderately funded and poorly attended.
FIGARO: Monica?
MON: Fill. The. Hole.
FIGARO: Giles?
GILES: I'm more of a fan of art people actually want to see. Cut, cut, cut I'm afraid.
FIGARO: Happy with that answer?
RON: Happy.

RON *gets up on stage and starts connecting a projector.*

LIZZIE: Ron, get off the stage.
GILES: Can we get security in here?

ACT THREE

MON: Distraction once again from the elites. We are not sheeple!
LIZZIE: What are you doing?
RON: I'm doing this for you, Lizzie.
LIZZIE: Doing what?
RON: Doing this for *love*!

> RON *switches on the projector, it spills over the audience. Everyone on stage tries to figure out what they are staring at—confused, aghast.*
>
> PHILLIPA *screams and points.*

PHILLIPA: PEEEEEEEEEEEEEEEEEEEEEEEEENIS!

> *Beat.*

FIGARO: Giles, is that your dick?

> *Beat.*

GILES: Yes.

> *Beat.*

LIZZIE: Wait, the picture above. Is that your arse, Ron?
RON: It most certainly is!

> WARREN, *sensing the need to cause a distraction, storms the stage.*

WARREN: Men are under attack! From feminists—
LIZZIE: Why are you sending a pic of your dick to my boyfriend?
WARREN: Cancel culture and unrealistic body expectations.
LIZZIE: Why is my boyfriend sending you a pic of his arse?

> LIZZIE *steps out from behind her platform.*

WARREN: Embrace your penises, brothers—no matter the size or curve—
GILES: I … I don't—
RON: Lizzie, I love you!
LIZZIE: Fuck off Ron.
WARREN: Old-fashioned words like 'monogamy' and 'faith' might be uncool nowadays.

> FIGARO *has taken the mic and is talking to the audience now.*

FIGARO: It's a question of character!

> LIZZIE *moves towards* GILES.

Of fidelity.

> MON *walks towards the audience and chants 'Fill the hole!'*

MON: Fill the hole!

GILES: I'm sorry, I'm really—

LIZZIE: What are you apologising for? I mean it's important for people to know whether their prospective president is a cheating prick with a cheating prick?

GILES: I don't feel comfortable.

LIZZIE: Fuuuuuuuck your comfort!

> LIZZIE *dives on* GILES, *knocking over the platform—she punches him in the face.* WARREN *drags* GILES *off and* PHILLIPA *drags* LIZZIE *off.*
>
> MON *stands on the adjudicator's platform and yells 'FILL THE HOLE!'*

3.

The Vice-Chancellor's office.

The VICE-CHANCELLOR *is behind the desk looking at a laptop:* WARREN *and* PHILLIPA *stand,* MON, LIZZIE *and* GILES *(with a black eye) sit.*

You can hear 'FILL THE HOLE!' again and again. Someone yells out 'Is that a sex thing?'

The video finishes. The VICE-CHANCELLOR *rubs her eyes.*

VICE-CHANCELLOR: So …

MON: I can explain—

VICE-CHANCELLOR: No. No. After that little brew-ha on the uni bar stage I am getting interview and meeting requests out my ears. It's not that I don't value transparency, I just like a quiet schedule. Following on from this public *display* and with a lot of consultation amongst the senior leadership team—

WARREN: I'd just like to jump in early and make this easy on everyone. Giles, you have made a mockery of the traditions and values I hold dear, consider this my resignation effective immediately.

WARREN *leaves.*

VICE-CHANCELLOR: What happened?

LIZZIE: Tensions were high because—

VICE-CHANCELLOR: I can see the video but what happened to the three of you? What has changed over the last month that turned you into animals?

GILES: I can explain.

VICE-CHANCELLOR: No. No. These are hypothetical questions. I thought maybe the pandemic would have created a circuit break for this kind of behaviour—a chance for pause, reflection and new ways emerging. Every few years a little bubble of fresh air rises to the surface, but instead you make the same self-interested mistakes again and again and again—proving those bubbles weren't fresh air, you know what they were? They. Were. Farts.

Beat.

Would you like a tissue, dear?

PHILLIPA: I'm so sorry. I quit. Lizzie? I quit!

PHILLIPA *leaves.*

VICE-CHANCELLOR: You're three very interesting, very smart, very connected individuals and when I saw you in here in these chairs a few weeks ago, I thought wow, maybe this is the year, maybe this is the cycle where the mud isn't slung to see what sticks, but rather an actual contest occurs, of ideas. I'm not naïve. I wasn't asking for *The Symposium* but I didn't expect *Wrestlemania*.

The VICE-CHANCELLOR *slams her laptop shut—they all sit up.*

I want you all to know this was a close call. A very, very, very close call. The senior leadership team, and the PR team for the university, begged me to cancel this election.

Beat.

I said no. Mainly because of the endless paperwork it would cause, but in a small part, I thought maybe this is a good reset point for the three of you. A good moment to look in the mirror and think about who you are and why you're doing this. I don't want to see you again until election day. The three of you can hand out how to votes, that's it. No other appearances. No other ploys. Your campaigns are your responsibility and it's on your shoulders whether this hundred-and-sixty-year-old institution remains active or not. My advice, not that any of you asked for it, but lay low, reflect and let what you've already done speak for itself. Now kindly, piss off.

    MON, GILES *and* LIZZIE *leave.*

    The VICE-CHANCELLOR *sits on her desk.*

    A moment.

    A knock on the door.

Not right now, thank you.

    A knock on the door.

I said—

    FIGARO *enters.*

    VICE-CHANCELLOR *and* FIGARO *lock eyes, the* VICE-CHANCELLOR *laughs.*

FIGARO: I've got a favour to ask.
VICE-CHANCELLOR: Oh Christ, you are good value.
FIGARO: Here's what I'm asking.
VICE-CHANCELLOR: You're serious?
FIGARO: Of course, why wouldn't I be?
VICE-CHANCELLOR: You know what you did?
FIGARO: I uncovered the Smaug's hoard of political journalism. One candidate was sending pictures of his dick to the other candidate's boyfriend.
VICE-CHANCELLOR: This is good to you?
FIGARO: Oh no, this is *gold*.
VICE-CHANCELLOR: Projecting the penis on the audience?
FIGARO: That's just the theatre of Ron.
VICE-CHANCELLOR: A lot of people want you out of this place, give me one good reason as to why I should let you stay.
FIGARO: I've got one … juicy answer.

    Beat.

VICE-CHANCELLOR: The straw?
FIGARO: Yeah.
VICE-CHANCELLOR: The picture of me using a *fucking* straw?

ACT THREE 75

FIGARO: See the thing is as my stories have gotten more and more traction—the *Guardian*, the *Financial Review*, *The Australian*—my stories have more heft. So what once would've hit an audience of two kids and their hamster, is now hitting about a million eyes and only god knows how many hamsters. I wonder what they'd all think about your little dalliance with Strawy McStrawface.

Beat.

VICE-CHANCELLOR: I don't push for your expulsion, and we're even.
FIGARO: Deal.

4.

The common room of the college. The loungeroom of the sharehouse.

Surrounded by the chaos: GILES *drinks whiskey straight from the bottle,* LIZZIE *calmly does the magic-eye crossword and drinking tea.*

The same blackboard exists in both rooms simultaneously.

WARREN *enters the sharehouse with a sense of curiosity and that of entering enemy territory.*

WARREN *knocks on something to get her attention.*

LIZZIE: Didn't hear you come in.
WARREN: Your housemates—
LIZZIE: Are both moving out. Yay. Come to laugh at me? Gloat? Mock? Cajole?
WARREN: Not at all.

Beat.

Mind if I sit down?
LIZZIE: Free country.
WARREN: Not if we keep letting other people illegally ... I mean, I've got something to say first, and I'd like to be standing if that's okay.
LIZZIE: Okay.
WARREN: What happened out there—
 On that stage—
 In front of all those people—
 I wanted to ... apologise. For whatever role our campaign played, for the personal role I played in enabling an environment where

that kind of disgusting exploitation and grubby politics prevented a chance for genuine discussion and debate.

LIZZIE: Wow.

WARREN: I mean every word.

> WARREN *and* LIZZIE *sit.* LIZZIE *holds her teacup.*

LIZZIE: Finding out in front of your whole university that your long-term boyfriend is cheating wasn't exactly high on my bucket list.

WARREN: Brutal.

LIZZIE: Violent.

WARREN: But … useful?

LIZZIE: Don't start.

WARREN: Hear me out. I've quit the other campaign because I morally object to what went down on that stage.

LIZZIE: Are you … ?

WARREN: I'll be in and out by the time you finish your tea.

> LIZZIE *sips.*

The palm card thing …

LIZZIE: Was a moment of weakness.

WARREN: Was an act of political genius. It proved to me that you're a candidate who would do anything to win this thing. I didn't have that in Giles, I think I have it in you.

> WARREN *walks to the blackboard.*

Good to see our pollsters were working for both sides.

LIZZIE: We were behind before the debate.

WARREN: You need sixty percent, you got fifty-five-point-five.

LIZZIE: Who knows how much I lost with that outburst?

WARREN: Did Phillipa ever consider … the elites?

LIZZIE: Never. Why would they vote for someone like me?

WARREN: Maybe they didn't realise they had so much in common.

LIZZIE: Are you suggesting a switch?

WARREN: Not entirely, no. Selectively. You're right, I'm not sure how much that outburst lost you with more progressive leaning …

> WARREN *circles 'persuadables' on the board.*

persuadables. Maybe it made you appear more human or totally unhinged.

LIZZIE: Thanks.
WARREN: But what do we know? It *might* have earned you some cred with some unexpected people.
LIZZIE: Because I beat up the guy who was sexting my partner?

Beat.

WARREN: Well ... yeah.
LIZZIE: It's that easy?
WARREN: Works really well for female country singers.
LIZZIE: People are going to vote for me because I look like a bigot?

Beat.

WARREN: Well ... yeah. Now I'm not saying they're going to hand it over. You'll have to meet with these people and assure them that you're aligned to their values.
LIZZIE: And if I'm not?
WARREN: Then they'll meet with me.
LIZZIE: What do I do?
WARREN: You need to go dark. Don't be seen or heard for the rest of the election.
LIZZIE: And you'll ... ?
WARREN: Maybe I run into someone at a rugby match. We start talking. Banter starts up.
'What's filling your day Waz?'
'I've been really inspired actually. But you don't want to hear, I don't want to bore you.'
But they do want to hear and I won't bore them. A vote here. A vote there. That's how we win this.
LIZZIE: That's a pretty small margin you're dancing on.
WARREN: Lucky I took three years of ballet, six years of tap.
LIZZIE: Why?
WARREN: Officially, Mum made me. Unofficially, I'm kind of good, hey.
LIZZIE: Why do you want to help?
WARREN: Why am I offering my assistance?
LIZZIE: Yeah. Why do you want me to win?
WARREN: Oh no. I don't. I want Giles to lose.

WARREN *drinks the last of* LIZZIE*'s tea.*

Sorry, lot of talking. Let me know what you want to do, it's up to you.

> WARREN *leaves,* LIZZIE *ponders.*

> PHILLIPA *enters the common room, knocks on something to get* GILES*'s attention.*

PHILLIPA: I just wanted to let you know that I'd stepped down from the other campaign.

GILES: That sucks, do you want to sit down? Can I get you anything?

> GILES *passes* PHILLIPA *a beer.*

PHILLIPA: I hate what Lizzie's become but what she's becoming is just you so you know what I want in my heart of hearts?

GILES: What's that?

> PHILLIPA *opens the beer with her teeth.*

PHILLIPA: I hope you both fucking fail. Thanks for the beer.

> *She leaves.*

> GILES *and* LIZZIE *sit down and stare at the blackboard. From somewhere we hear …*

TASH: He is driven by proving everyone wrong.

FIGARO: Immovable object.

TASH: She is driven by showing everyone she's right.

FIGARO: Meets unstoppable force.

> GILES *stands up and circles 'The Involved'.* LIZZIE *stands up and circles 'The Elite'—they both look at the board.*

MON: Fill the hole.

ELISE: Is that a sex thing?

5.

The student newspaper.

ELISE *and* ANDY *are sitting at the table.*

ANDY: This feels important.

ELISE: What does?

ANDY: This moment.

ELISE: Momentous? Moments are momentous.

ACT THREE

ANDY: Things are changing underfoot. Thank you, this moment feels momentous. We're on the edge of something big.

ELISE: He's gone, surely?

ANDY: If he can just be ousted on a whim, who's next?

ELISE: This isn't burning down the Reichstag—he projected a dick on an audience, pretty open-and-shut case.

ANDY: The fact the VC can kick out someone without any due process.

ELISE: We don't know there hasn't been any due process.

ANDY: I knew you'd side with the brownshirts.

ELISE: What brownshirts? It's his debate, remember. All I know is I've thrown parties so I know what it takes to not end up in a fight. And my parties have goon of fortune.

ANDY: Now what?

ELISE: I'm ready to—

> FIGARO *bursts through the door carrying a juice—he puts it down and puts up the images he took in the last montage up on the board.*

FIGARO: Sorry, I'm late.

ANDY: What the hell is happening?

ELISE: We thought you were sacked.

FIGARO: Ha. LOL. I needed juice.

> *Finishing the photos on the wall,* FIGARO *faces the journalists for the first time.*

Up to this point you had pretty free rein over what you covered, how you covered it, but we're going to be streamlining some of those sections and practices into a more focused bulletin—emphasis on the *bullet*. Under a new remit we will be exclusively student politics—people want to see the sausage getting made so we're going from the paddock to the saleyards to the abattoirs to the butchers to the barbeque to the plate on this. It's what gets the hits, it's what other publications want to reprint, it's what people outside of campus want to read. So in simple economic terms, we will create a supply to meet that demand.

ANDY: What about sport?

FIGARO: No more sport.

ANDY: I only need a few more articles for my portfolio.

FIGARO: General rule is if we can't be the only player in the arena, and thus the strongest gladiator by default, that section is cut.

ANDY: That's not how sports work. I'd know that because I'm the sports writer. This is unfair.

FIGARO: Same goes for Elise for your social events and student profiles too—too much effort for too little eyeballs. Any other questions?

Pause.

ELISE: Why weren't you fired?

FIGARO: What?

ELISE: You caused the debate debacle, why weren't you fired?

FIGARO: Elise, I can see you're upset about intersex netball being cut, but the decision's been made. You can get on board or you can disembark, they're your options.

ELISE: The student in student journalism is important. It's the gig, it's the readers, it's the writers. We're learning, we're students, and I'm not sure what it'll be, but I hope when your shitshow here is over and you're looking at what's left after all this, you've learned something.

ELISE *leaves.*

FIGARO: Didn't even have to sack her? That's easy. Now we've got the last few days of the campaign coming up so I want eyes on—

ANDY: It was really good. Really bloody good.

FIGARO: What was?

ANDY: The women's rugby. Would never have given it a chance if it wasn't for this place. Good luck putting out a paper when you don't even know how the fucking printer works.

ANDY *leaves.*

FIGARO *is alone with everything he ever wanted. How does he feel about this? He avoids the thought by picking up his phone and calling a number.*

FIGARO *leans into the phone—*

FIGARO: I know you've stopped taking my calls but that doesn't mean this is over, this election may be nearing its end, but I've only just begun. I don't need this newspaper for what I'm about to do next but I do need you to know one thing: you've created a monster and I intend on being monstrous.

ACT FOUR: THE ELECTION

1.

Dawn.

The main thoroughfare of the university with the bell tower looming—
TASH *is inside.*

As the sun rises, we see the place come to life.

Groundskeepers mow and rake.

Cleaners pick up the detritus of the previous day: coffee cups, kebab wrappers, beer bottles.

The place becomes fresh. Voting booths are set up.

The lounge room. WARREN *is there, sipping from a sports bottle.* LIZZIE *is at the blackboard.*

GILES *drinks a coffee and rubs a headache from his forehead.*

FIGARO *does full calisthenics.*

The bell tower rings and the campaigning can begin.

MON *covers the back wall with orange 'Fill The Hole' posters over the following:*

ii.

LIZZIE *writes 'Religious Groups' on the blackboard.*

WARREN *walks with a nun, a man in a kippah and a woman in a hijab. He hands her a Bible, the nun opens it and there's an 'I'm With Lizzie!' pamphlet inside.*

FIGARO *takes a picture.*

iii.

GILES *talks with a member of the book group—he passes her a 'Giles!' pamphlet. He walks of. The book-group member scrunches up the paper and throws it away.*

FIGARO *takes a picture.*

iv.

KEV *meets with members of the rugby team, the basketball team and some fencers. He holds a box.*

KEV: It's a simple message guys but it really speaks to what's at stake in this election. Sports. Fill the hole. Find your hole: whether that be the tryline, the hoop or the … other guy dressed like a beekeeper. Filling your hole is about achieving your goal and not letting anyone get in your way.

    He hands out 'how-to-votes'.

v.

LIZZIE *writes 'Pro-Life 4 Lyf'.*

WARREN *walks with a student holding a placard with a fetus on it—he's in animated discussion then he passes him an 'I'm With Lizzie!' pamphlet.*

FIGARO *takes a picture.*

vi.

GILES *is in a lab coat with a group of others in the same—he passes over a 'Giles!' pamphlet. Nobody takes it.*

FIGARO *takes a picture.*

vii.

STEW *holds a skull in his hand. He wears an orange T-shirt with 'Fill The Hole' on it.*

STEW: To fill, or not to fill, that is the question:
    Whether 'tis nobler in the mind to suffer
    The bump-ed toes of faulty roadwork,
    Or to take up arms against a road of troubles
    And with spade in hand end them. To die—to trip,
    No more; and by a trip to say we end
    The heart-ache and the hundred unnatural shocks
    That open toed feet are aired to: 'tis the fate
    Devoutely to be wish'd. To slip, to trip,
    To trip perchance to fall—ay there's the rub:
    Pause.
Vote Monica.

ACT FOUR

viii.

LIZZIE *writes 'Convoy For Coal'.*

WARREN *wears a hard hat and cuts a ribbon.*

FIGARO *takes a picture.*

ix.

GILES *wears a vest. He yells with a bunch of other people holding pieces of paper in their hands. They see who it is and shuffle along and leave him by himself.*

FIGARO *takes a picture.*

x.

LIZZIE *writes down 'Illuminati'.*

WARREN *meets with a bunch of men in monks' robes—they drink.*

FIGARO *takes a picture.*

PHILLIPA *enters the sharehouse with a cardboard box of belongings, she shakes her head and walks off.*

LIZZIE *looks at the board before tearing it into pieces.*

xi.

GILES, *by himself, wanders around with a sign saying 'Giles!'*

FIGARO *takes a picture.*

xii.

HANYA *is with a bunch of women playing beer-pong.*

HANYA: Filling the hole is really a feminist undertaking. It's not saying we need anyone else to help, it's not saying we need anyone else's permission, it's about empowerment and reclaiming what is owed to us—our right to fill the hole. Who's with me?

    They drink.

xiii.

LIZZIE, *trying to add up some maths on the broken blackboard, looks behind her …*

GILES, *sitting on the ground dejected, looks up ...*
The spectre of Mon covers the back wall of the theatre.

2.

A screen falls.
A giant QR code fills it.
The audience is asked to turn their phones on, scan the code and vote.
A red countdown timer begins in the corner, informing the audience that polls close in three minutes.
Once the three minutes are over, the curtain rises.

3.

Dusk of election day.
The campaigners have dispersed, the detritus of election day lingers—streamers, posters and coffee cups cover the ground.
The voting booths are being packed up.
GILES *sits on the edge of the stage with a six-pack of beer cans, utterly exhausted.*
LIZZIE *enters with a CBD pen and sits on the opposite end of the stage.*
They each know the other one is there but hope they weren't noticed—too exhausted to move on.
They sit in silence for a moment.
GILES *opens a can and the noise breaks the tension between them. They look at each other—small smiles of rivals.*
Eyes back to the front, without looking at each other, is the only way they can talk ...

LIZZIE: Did you ever sleep together?
GILES: Me and Ron? No.
    Beat.
  We messaged a couple of times on the app.
LIZZIE: Send pictures of your junk?

GILES: That one time. We mainly just talked. He was the only one too. But no, we never slept together.

Beat.

He never mentioned he had a girlfriend, I mean I didn't expect him to have one so I guess that assumption's on me. I just mean he never mentioned you.

LIZZIE: Did you mention your girlfriend?

GILES: Ex-girlfriend. Kind of. I don't know. When she left it was hazy how—

LIZZIE: Did you mention Gert?

GILES: We spend as much time talking about our girlfriends on the gay dating app as you'd expect. It was all very pretend in a way. Felt good though. Maybe I'll look into what that is one day.

Beat.

Next time, if there is a next time, I will be more up front about my relationship status.

LIZZIE: Promise?

GILES: Promise.

Pause.

LIZZIE: I'm sorry for punching you.

GILES: Are you kidding me? Black eye? Every little boy's dream.

GILES *stands up, grabs another beer and moves to* LIZZIE.

LIZZIE: I'm sorry.

GILES: I'm sorry too.

LIZZIE *accepts the beer, opens it and they cheers.*

How'd you go?

LIZZIE: Today? I have no fucking idea. You?

GILES: Oh in the bag.

LIZZIE: Really?

GILES: Totally. Strong turnout from the base, persuadables were persuaded, and the exit polls indicate that I've got no fucking idea either.

LIZZIE: Lot of orange.

GILES: Last few days, a lot of fucking orange.

LIZZIE: I thought I was being paranoid.
GILES: No, she tapped into something.
LIZZIE: She did.
GILES: What was that?
LIZZIE: She knew why she was running. She had a reason.
GILES: What was yours?
LIZZIE: Super simple. I was asked.
GILES: That's it?
LIZZIE: That's really kind of it.
GILES: Me too. I hadn't even considered it.
LIZZIE: Then in the space of a month that's your entire world.
GILES: It was like a fungus,
LIZZIE: A virus,
GILES: A monster consuming everything
LIZZIE: And everyone in its wake.
GILES: It's like I had no say in it.

>*They laugh.*
>
>*They keep laughing.*
>
>*They are both emotionally and physically wrecked and the only thing left to do is laugh.*
>
>*On their backs, spent—they've got nothing else to give.*
>
>*A clump-clump-clump noise can be heard—both turn around. It's* MON. *She smiles.*

MON: Are these up for grabs?

>GILES *throws* MON *a beer and looks around.*

Wild huh? I didn't think when I met you in that office, it would lead to … all this.
GILES: Got a little out of hand.
LIZZIE: Yup.
MON: Fun but.
GILES: Ha.
LIZZIE: Sure.
LIZZIE: How long have you got left? In the boot?
MON: Get it off next week, just as I'm getting used to it. It's kind of my brand now. Will people recognise me without it?

ACT FOUR

GILES: I think people know what you look like now Monica.
MON: You reckon?
LIZZIE: I don't think that's going to be a problem.

> *They watch as* MON *struggles to sit down—*LIZZIE *helps her sit.*
>
> *All three of them sip their beers.*

MON: I was wondering hey, if—

> MON *knocks wood.*

I win. What if day one: I just fill the hole? What do I do then?
LIZZIE: There are always other holes.
GILES: Deep.
MON: LOL. Deep holes.
GILES: Quick question: 'fill the hole'?
LIZZIE: I wanted to ask this too.
GILES/LIZZIE: Is it a sex thing?
MON: Well …

> *Their phones beep.*
>
> MON, LIZZIE *and* GILES *get out their phones.*

LIZZIE: This is it.
GILES: Shit.
MON: I can't look.
GILES: I don't really want to know.

> *They all take a deep breath in.*

MON: Break a leg!
LIZZIE: Chookas.
GILES: Good luck.
MON: Check at the same time?
LIZZIE: Three,
GILES: Two,
MON: One.

> *They open their messages. Their faces are lit up.*

4.

A projection of a giant fig slams against the back wall.

The sound of glass smashing, bombs crashing and guns firing. Stock footage of war, unrest and puppies.

'FIG'S FACTS!'

FIGARO: Welcome back to Fig's facts. No lies, no spin, just …

'FIG'S FACTS!'

Another camera angle.

I am excited today. This is an election that has rocked the university to its core. We've been gifted a new president—a maverick, an original, someone who tells it like it is, doesn't read off a teleprompter, they're self-made but are they ready to take control of the chaos and darkness that reigns? *My opinion, dear viewer?*

Another camera angle.

Of course not!

'FIG FACT!' slams onto the screen.

But let's give them the benefit of the doubt, let's cut them a chance, the people have spoken, but do the people have a good singing voice? We cut live to the victory speech now.

The VICE-CHANCELLOR *stands behind a lectern. Next to them, seated is the winner of the election. They are hollowed out, confused.*

VICE-CHANCELLOR: Today is a momentous day, a turning of the page, a falling of a leaf then turning that leaf over from an old autumn to a new spring. We have here today a new young leader who continues a long tradition, a proud tradition. I'm reminded of the great Paul Keating when he said—

The camera zooms in closer and closer onto the face of the winner. The VICE-CHANCELLOR*'s voice morphs demonically.*

I want to do you slowly.

EPILOGUE

The Vice-Chancellor's Office.

VICE-CHANCELLOR: Well, that was a lot.

TASH: I had fun.

VICE-CHANCELLOR: Well, you weren't really a part of it.

TASH: It's amazing what *not* smashing three Red Bulls first thing in the morning does for your health.

VICE-CHANCELLOR: Best stick to tea.

TASH: And juice.

VICE-CHANCELLOR: Of course.

TASH: I told you the watermelon was good, remember?

Pause.

VICE-CHANCELLOR: And the thesis? All finished?

TASH: My supervisor thinks there's enough for a PhD.

VICE-CHANCELLOR: Ancient history, right?

TASH: Lessons from the Bronze Age collapse.

VICE-CHANCELLOR: And were there any?

TASH: The ancient kingdoms of the Mediterranean—all interconnected through trade and cultural piggybacking, all stalled. The current theory is that a combination of climate change; drought and famine; internal fractures led to the eventual collapse of these first great civilisations.

VICE-CHANCELLOR: Powder keg huh?

TASH: Of sorts.

VICE-CHANCELLOR: What set it off?

TASH: An outside invader.

Beat. It dawns on the VICE-CHANCELLOR:

VICE-CHANCELLOR: But … wait. How did you know Elizabeth and Giles would run?

TASH: I told them they should.

VICE-CHANCELLOR: But Monica decided on the spot. I was there when she nominated.

TASH: Well, there weren't a lot of decisions left.

VICE-CHANCELLOR: How could you possibly know Monica would run?

TASH: I knew whoever mustered the guts to complain directly to you about that hole would be the kind of person my thesis needed. If it wasn't her, there would've been someone else.
VICE-CHANCELLOR: That's a lot of coincidences.
TASH: Not at all.
VICE-CHANCELLOR: What about the hole?
TASH: I dug it.
VICE-CHANCELLOR: You what?
TASH: I dug the hole outside her bus stop.
VICE-CHANCELLOR: You're a …
TASH: First-class honours student?
VICE-CHANCELLOR: A complete psycho!
TASH: It took a psychotic episode to get to this point but the clarity I achieved is quite sane. Collapse is only scary for those who the system is currently working for.
VICE-CHANCELLOR: You were president, it was clearly working for you. It was working for me!
TASH: I've spent my year as president prevented from doing anything because there's zero incentive for anybody to change anything. Everyone's in a race to the bottom over who can be the worst possible person the most amount of the time, and still get your vote because you don't *really* have a choice.
VICE-CHANCELLOR: So you sabotage the entire process?
TASH: What you're suggesting is unethical and I got ethics approval. All I did was set up an experiment, let it run and observe the results.
VICE-CHANCELLOR: Well … fuck your experiment!

> *The* VICE-CHANCELLOR *regains her composure—stands up, picks up both teacups.*

Thanks for coming in today, Tash, and I wish you the best in your future studies.
TASH: Oh I'm not going to do a PhD—I figure I should try out my thesis in the real world.
VICE-CHANCELLOR: Well, whatever it is you do I hope I never see you again.
TASH: Oh I'm only just getting started.

THE END

CANBERRA YOUTH THEATRE PRESENTS

HOW TO VOTE!

OR, THE REPERCUSSIONS OF POLITICAL AMBITION AND PERSONAL RIVALRIES WITHIN STUDENT LEADERSHIP AND MEDIA ORGANISATIONS IN THE CONTEXT OF THE POST-COVID-19 NEOLIBERAL UNIVERSITY INSTITUTION

BY JULIAN LARNACH

WORLD PREMIERE
7 – 10 SEPTEMBER 2022
THE PLAYHOUSE THEATRE – CANBERRA THEATRE CENTRE

CAST

THE SHARE HOUSE
LIZZIE	CAITLIN BAKER
KEV	TIM CUSACK
PHILLIPA	JASMINE ATKINS

THE COLLEGE
GILES	MATT WHITE
WARREN	NICHOLAS BERMINGHAM
HANYA	RAHEL ALEMSEGED

THE ALARUM NEWSPAPER
FIGARO	JACK SHANAHAN
ELISE	THEA JADE
ANDY	MISCHA RIPPON

THE STUDENT DRAMA SOCIETY
RON	BLUE HYSLOP
STEW	CALLUM DOHERTY

THE TOWNIES
MON	ELLA BUCKLEY

VICE CHANCELLOR	TRACY NOBLE
TASH	JOANNA RICHARDS
PRATCHETT	CLAIRE IMLACH
GERT	MARTHA RUSSELL

ENSEMBLE	ASHLEIGH BUTLER
	JESSICA GOODING
	QUINN GOODWIN
	BREANNA KELLY
	YVETTE MPINGA
	BEN O'LOUGHLIN
	CAMERON ROSE
	EMILY SMITH
	THOMAS WARBURTON
	SAAR WESTON

CREATIVE TEAM

DIRECTOR	LUKE ROGERS
LIGHTING DESIGNER	ANTONY HATELEY
COSTUME DESIGNER	HELEN WOJTAS
SOUND DESIGNER	PATRICK HAESLER
VIDEO DESIGNER	ETHAN HAMILL
ASSISTANT DIRECTOR	SOPHIE TALLIS
STAGE MANAGER	RHILEY WINNETT
ASSISTANT STAGE MANAGERS	STEPHANIE EVANS
	KATE MCDONALD
	ROWENA MCPHEE
	ASHLEY POPE
COSTUME ASSISTANT	RHIANNON ROBERTS

ACKNOWLEDGEMENTS

We greatly acknowledge the support of the ACT Government through artsACT, and Ainslie and Gorman Arts Centres.

This production is supported by Canberra Theatre Centre, as part of a commitment to nurturing the young and emerging artists of the ACT.

Special thanks to The Museum of Australian Democracy at Old Parliament House.

Thanks to Stephen Crossley, Elections ACT, Jess Kirby, and all of the artists that have generously contributed to the creative development workshops of this play.

OUR PARTNERS

Canberra Youth Theatre acknowledges the Ngunnawal people as the traditional custodians of the lands on which we collaborate, share stories and create art. We pay respect to their Elders, past and present and emerging, and recognise their enduring culture and contribution to our community. We celebrate their rich history of over 60,000 years of storytelling, and are privileged and grateful to share our stories here. This is Ngunnawal country. Always was. Always will be.

50 YEARS YOUNG

Canberra Youth Theatre is one of the leading youth arts companies in Australia.

We develop opportunities for young people to collaborate, develop their artistic skills and create pathways to the professional arts sector.

We advocate for and amplify the voices of young people, providing a space for them to discover and express their creative selves.

We produce powerful theatre where young artists ignite urgent conversations, challenge the forces that shape them, and invite us to see the world from new perspectives.

Over our 50 year history, we have collaborated with thousands of young artists through productions, workshops, creative developments and community events. We have created works in our major theatres, public spaces, and national cultural institutions. We have toured around the country, and internationally.

Canberra Youth Theatre has grown and evolved significantly over the past five decades, constantly responding to the passions and perspectives of generations of young people, and adapting to changes in the way we create and experience live performance. We remain at the forefront of Australian youth theatre practice, creating innovative, accessible and challenging opportunities for young people to access and engage in professional-quality theatrical experiences.

Canberra Youth Theatre has proven experience commissioning, developing, producing and promoting new Australian writing. From Debra Oswald's now Australian classic *Dags*, and works by writers Tommy Murphy, Mary Rachel Brown, Lachlan Philpott, Angela Bezien, Liv Hewson, Ross Mueller, Emily Sheehan, Jessica Bellamy, and Tasnim Hossain, we have nurtured new voices and commissioned professional artists to create acclaimed works for young people.

We continue to nurture and develop young people, giving them a place to belong, to share their voice, and to inspire audiences of all ages.

THE VOICE OF YOUTH EXPRESSED THROUGH INTELLIGENT AND CHALLENGING THEATRE

PLAYWRIGHT'S NOTE

When I was at university, I was involved in student politics – affectionately known as stupol. Okay, involved doesn't quite cover the fanaticism and verve I brought to proceedings. I ran for and was elected an editor of the student newspaper, I sat on the Student Representative Council and I spent way too much time wearing primary coloured t-shirts splashed with slogans trying to get friends elected to the student union board of directors. I was motivated by equal parts ambition and spite, and was exhilarated by the idea of skipping class in order to change my little sandstone world.

When I started talking to Luke at Canberra Youth Theatre about what a work about young people engaging in democracy would look like, the flashbacks began. The midnight chalking to the sound of the Kooks, the handing out fliers wearing a haircut I'd seen Justin Timberlake rock in a film clip and the empassioned speeches given to lecture halls in skinny jeans I couldn't squat in for fear of a crotch rip. The dramatic form of these memories didn't take shape until a visit to the Museum of Australian Democracy at Old Parliament House. It was here I heard with fresh ears (and less form fitting pants) the words: 'student politics'. Rather than describing the environment, I heard 'student' as a qualifier. As a raison d'etre for experimentation. As an excuse for bad behaviour.

Student politics, student media, student theatre. These are the realms where some of our great politicians, journalists and artists began their careers – leaving indelible marks and long shadows on campuses around the country. I dipped my toe into each of these pools during my tertiary education and I felt first hand the power of imitation in these waters. As a young person, you put on the clothes, you get the haircut, you listen to the music that you're supposed to until you find the ones that fit you. This play is an attempt to capture the intensity of emotion in this specific lacuna – the keenly felt sting of reaching for adulthood while being reminded you're just a student, the bad taste in your mouth as you attempt to be a maker while keenly aware you only have the skillset of a faker.

Returning to this particular world a decade later with Luke and the amazing young artists at Canberra Youth Theatre, I found that even though the music, haircuts and fashion had changed, the same awkward pulse was still beating beneath the surface. This play is dedicated to my stupol comrades in arms – those who sought out functions for the debate as much as the free beer, who embraced the co- more than the -curricular and realise to this day that's where the real knowledge was gleaned.

Julian Larnach

DIRECTOR'S NOTE

Not long after I started with Canberra Youth Theatre in 2019, I visited the Museum of Australian Democracy at Old Parliament House. I was particularly intrigued by their *Democracy: Are You In?* exhibit, exploring democracy in action and what motivates young people to recognise the power of their voice. The conversations started flowing with our young artists about how they felt living in our nation's capital – the political centre of Australia, surrounded by government institutions with the House on the hill at its core. Did this make them more politically engaged, or apathetic towards our democratic systems? As a company, I wanted us to look at how young people viewed the culture of politics, what was behind their growing distrust towards political systems, and the issues that activated them to advocate for social change.

Canberra is also a university town, so before long we started to talk about what happens when the word 'student' is placed before things like politics, journalism, and theatre. A university feels like a microcosm of our society; a place where we learn about the arts, philosophy, technology and science, but also how to basically function living out of home. We discover our tribes, often stay in our social bubbles, and declare that we're going to take over the world. We party hard, fall in love, mess up, think that we know it all, realise that we never will, but remain determined to challenge the establishment and make things better – all whilst under the pressure of having to get our essay in on time.

I brought Julian on board to join me in these conversations, and throughout many workshops and creative developments with our young artists – culminating in a staged reading in the House of Representatives at Old Parliament House last year – here we are with the world premiere of a new Australian play on The Playhouse stage.

I am proud that we have created an epic work for a huge ensemble of emerging artists; a satirical play that delves into the cut-throat world of student politics, about what drives our ambition for power, and the lengths we are prepared to go to hold onto it.

Thank you to the team at the Canberra Theatre Centre who have generously supported this production as part of their commitment to nurturing the young and emerging artists of the ACT.

How To Vote! is one of many new Australian plays that have been commissioned by Canberra Youth Theatre. The stories of young people are at the heart of our work, and we are committed to investing in the creation of new works, and nurturing the development of our emerging artists. Now more than ever, we need to advocate for the voice of our young people, and celebrate what our youth arts sector is capable of.

Luke Rogers

CREATIVE TEAM

JULIAN LARNACH | PLAYWRIGHT

Julian Larnach is a Sydney-based playwright and the Literary Associate at Griffin Theatre Company. 2022 sees the premieres of his stage adaptation of Favel Parrett's award winning novel *Past The Shallows* for Australian Theatre for Young People and Archipelago Productions (Tasmania), and a new large-cast political comedy for Canberra Youth Theatre, *How To Vote!* He is currently under commission with Bell Shakespeare for a new cycle of history plays and is developing a new work for Griffin Theatre Company. Julian has had seasons of work produced and toured by the Australian Theatre for Young People, Outback Theatre for Young People, Darlinghurst Theatre Company and the National Theatre of Parramatta. Julian's plays have been shortlisted for Griffin Theatre Company's Lysicrates Prize, the Griffin Award for Playwriting, the Edward Albee Scholarship, and the Queensland Premier's Drama Award. He was an Affiliate Writer for Griffin Theatre Company in 2013, Resident Playwright at the Australian Theatre for Young People in 2015, and was a member of Sydney Theatre Company's inaugural Emerging Writers Group from 2017–2019.

LUKE ROGERS | DIRECTOR

Luke Rogers is the Artistic Director & CEO of Canberra Youth Theatre, a graduate of NIDA (Directing), Theatre Nepean (Acting), and the Artistic Director of Stories Like These. Previous positions: Theatre Manager of New Theatre, Artistic Director of The Spare Room, and a Resident Studio Artist at Griffin Theatre Company. Directing credits include: *Dags, Two Twenty Somethings Decide Never To Be Stressed About Anything Ever Again. Ever., Little Girls Alone in the Woods, Normal, Possibility, Collapse* (Canberra Youth Theatre), *In Real Life* (Darlinghurst Theatre), *Blink, MinusOneSister, Fireface, The Last Five Years, The Carnivores* (Stories Like These), *Play House* (NIDA), *The Pillowman, Waiting For Godot, Don Juan in Soho, Art is a Weapon, After The End, Blasted* (New Theatre), *100 Reasons For War, Love and Information, Spring Awakening, A Midsummer Night's Dream, Shakespeare's Women, Shoot/Get Treasure/Repeat* (AFTT), *Lysistrata, The Burial At Thebes, Pool (No Water), 4.48 Psychosis, Eyes To The Floor* (Sydney Theatre School), *A Midsummer Night's Dream, Mr Marmalade* (CQUniversity), *Macbeth, Cyberbile, Embers* (AIM Dramatic Arts), *Two Weeks With The Queen* (Mountains Youth Theatre). Tour Director: *The Witches* (Griffin). Assistant Director: *Eight Gigabytes of Hardcore Pornography* (Griffin), *Story of the Red Mountains* (NIDA), *The Boys* (Griffin), *Steel Magnolias* (Blackbird Productions), *Assassins, The Crucible* (New Theatre). Luke is currently studying for an MFA in Cultural Leadership at NIDA.

ANTONY HATELEY | LIGHTING DESIGNER

Antony Hateley is a lighting designer from the UK now based in the ACT, working in the dance and theatre industry. His work has featured both nationally and internationally and has covered dance, theatre, opera, fashion, and the corporate sector. He trained in fine art at University of Central England specialising in film and sculpture. A selection of the artists and organisations Antony has previously worked for includes Rambert, Ivan Putrov, Sadler's Wells Theatre, Dance Art Foundation, London College of Fashion, Viviana Durante Company, Botis Seva, Martin Creed, Van Huynh Company, Breakin' Convention, East London Dance, Akademi, Boy Blue Entertainment, Company Decalage and Avant Garde Dance. In addition to lighting design Antony has been frequently involved in artistic development programs providing nurture and support for new and emerging artists through organisations in the UK such as Sadler's Wells Theatre, East London Dance and Breakin' Convention. For Canberra Youth Theatre, Antony has designed *Dags, Two Twenty Somethings Decide Never To Be Stressed About Anything Ever Again. Ever.*, and *Little Girls Alone in the Woods*.

HELEN WOJTAS | COSTUME DESIGNER

Helen Wojtas is a Canberra based Costumier, who specialises in costumes for dance, circus and other movement based performance disciplines. She graduated in 2015 from the Western Australian Academy of Performing Arts (Costume Construction), and is currently studying an MBA (Arts and Cultural Management). After a brief stint in Melbourne (*Spring Awakening* (StageArt, 2017), *Anna Bolena* (Melbourne Opera, 2016), Helen returned to her hometown. Since her return to Canberra, Helen has designed costumes for *Happy Birthday Wanda June* (Canberra Repertory Society 2018), *Journey in my Hat* (Warehouse Circus 2018), *Giselle, Act 2* (Dance Development Centre 2018), *Circus De Light* (Warehouse Circus 2019), *Quizzic Alley - the Great Wizard Ball* (Warehouse Circus 2019), *Little Girls Alone in the Woods* (Canberra Youth Theatre 2021), and *Urinetown* (Heartstrings 2022). Helen continues to create bespoke costumes for dance, circus, and ice dance performers in the Canberra region. Helen is thrilled to create the world of the large ensemble cast, and reminisce about her own undergrad days (it's totally not set at the ANU, right?).

CREATIVE TEAM

PATRICK HAESLER | SOUND DESIGNER

Patrick Haesler is a composer, performer, sound designer and recording artist from Canberra. Beginning as a trumpeter, Patrick has since branched into numerous musical fields, drawing influences from jazz and progressive music. In 2018 Patrick entered the world of theatre, acting as musical director for ANU's Arts Revue. Since then, he has reprised this role, as well as composing music and designing sound for several theatre productions. These include: *It's Not Creeepy If They're Hot*, *Macbeth*, *The Tempest*, *Twelfth Night*, and *Dracula*. In 2021, Patrick's soundtrack for *Macbeth* was released as *The Scottish Album (Original Theatre Soundtrack)*, featuring a host of talentred guest musicians and collaborators performing original compositions. Patrick's experience with a wide variety of musical genres, ensembles and production techniques have made him a versatile creative in the world of music and sound. For Canberra Youth Theatre, Patrick was the sound designer for *The Initiation*, and is also currently designing sound for *Soul Trading*.

ETHAN HAMILL | VIDEO DESIGNER

Ethan Hamill is an emerging theatre practitioner, who specialises in lighting design, video design, and production management. Ethan's journey in the arts industry begun in 2014 with Canberra Youth Theatre where he worked on *Collapse, I'm Me, Possibility* (2019), *Fading* (2018) *Versions of Us* (2017), and *The Verbatim Project* (2016). Ethan is currently in his third and final year of study at NIDA, where he is doing a Bachelor of Fine Arts in Technical Theatre and Stage Management. Ethan strives to keep up with new and emerging technology and is always trying to bring these technologies into theatre and live events. This has led him to have the opportunity to work on several theatrical shows, dance events, live concerts, and installations. Ethan's recent credits include production manager for *Falsettos* (2022), lighting designer for *Too Human* (2022), *The Life That I Gave You* (2022), co-lighting designer for *Scooby Doo and The Creepy Carnival* (2021), and co-video designer for *Eat Me* (STC/NIDA Collaboration). Ethan is excited to be back with Canberra Youth Theatre as the video designer for *How to Vote!* and is looking forward to working with the rest of his fellow creatives to produce this work.

SOPHIE TALLIS | ASSISTANT DIRECTOR

Sophie Tallis is an emerging theatre maker and director. Sophie is a Resident Artist with Canberra Youth Theatre for 2022, and was the assistant director on *Dags*. She has previously directed *Love and Information* (2021) and *It's Not Creepy If They're Hot* (2019) for the National University Theatre Society, and performed in a range of shows while at university including the ANU Law Revue, *Pygmalion*, *The Island of Doctor Moreau*, *The History Boys*, and *The Importance of Being Earnest* for which she was nominated for a CAT award (2018). In addition, Sophie was the President of the ANU Shakespeare Society in 2020 having previously been the founding secretary. Sophie is currently completing her honours thesis in Screen Studies at the Australian National University, and has written on films and theatre for a range of local and national publications.

RHILEY WINNETT | STAGE MANAGER

Rhiley Winnett has stage managed with Canberra Youth Theatre on a variety of shows over the last few years including *Normal, Little Girls Alone in the Woods, Two Twenty Somethings Decide Never to be Stressed About Anything Ever Again. Ever., Dags,* and *The Initiation*. Rhiley has also stage managed Echo Theatre Company's *Wolf Lullaby*, three shows at their previous college, and works at Erindale Theatre. Rhiley is grateful for the opportunity to work with so many talented young actors (even if some are older than them) and is constantly inspired by their abilities. Rhiley is passionate about continuing to work with youth performers as they will change the theatre industry, and more importantly, the world. Being in charge of such a large group of talented people has been terrifying, but Rhiley has done their best in helping create a safe and efficient environment for them to learn and rehearse in. The show has been absolutely fantastic to be a part of and they're so grateful to everyone on the team.

CREATIVE TEAM

STEPHANIE EVANS | ASSISTANT STAGE MANAGER

Like most law students, Stephanie Evan's creative outlet is university theatre. Having dabbled in stage management, producing & directing, Steph is really keen to explore theatre outside of a university setting and work with the incredible team of actors & creatives on *How to Vote!*

KATE MCDONALD | ASSISTANT STAGE MANAGER

Kate McDonald has been involved in the production side of theatre since moving to Canberra. She has been backstage in many university productions at the Australian National University, most notably producing Wright & Bruce Hall's *Romeo and Juliet* (2020), being head of production for ANU Shakespeare Society's *The Tempest* (2021), and directing and producing the National University Theatre Society's *Dracula* (2022). She has also done costume, set and production design for multiple shows since 2019. This is her first show with Canberra Youth Theatre.

ROWENA MCPHEE | ASSISTANT STAGE MANAGER

Rowena McPhee used to perform on stage, but a few years ago, made a permanent switch to the dark side and have been working backstage ever since. After many years producing, directing, marketing, stage managing and socialising with ANU student theatre, Rowena is excited to be working with Canberra Youth Theatre, not least because it has provided a welcome distraction from their Honours thesis. Hopefully after working on *How To Vote!*, they'll finally know what to do when the next election comes around.

ASHLEY POPE | ASSISTANT STAGE MANAGER

Ashley Pope has been an assistant stage manager for Canberra Youth Theatre on Little Girls Alone in the Woods, Two Twenty Somethings Decide Never be Stressed About Anything Ever Again. Ever, and Dags. She has also been assistant stage manager on Rope at Canberra REP Theatre, as well as lighting technician on The Penelopiad for Papermoon Theatre.

RHIANNON ROBERTS | COSTUME ASSISTANT

Rhiannon Roberts is a second-year student studying fashion design and merchandising at the Canberra Institute of Technology in Canberra. Having developed a love for making clothes in high school, she began to delve into the worlds of cosplay and later costume-making in college, being fascinated by it as a means of expression and story-telling. Rhiannon was immediately drawn in by this play's witty story and fun character relationships, and couldn't wait to help to bring them and the story to life on stage through costume. After graduating, she hopes to continue to develop her skills in the realm of costume, with the dream of attending the National Institute of Dramatic Arts one day, and maybe even making it to the musical scene in America. Her other dream is to attend New York Comic Con dressed as her favourite anime character.

CAST

RAHEL ALEMSEGED | HANYA

Rahel Alemseged first began training in acting at the age of 11. She has since performed in a number of local theatre productions, including *Mystery on the Orient Express*, and *Pygmalion*. Rahel has completed up to grade 9 Speech and Drama examinations through Trinity Guildhall London. After a short hiatus during university, she is glad to be immersing herself in the Canberra arts community, having acted in many short films, and recently completing the film adaptation of Maura Pierlot's play *Fragments*, with director Declan Shrubb in March 2022.

JASMINE ATKINS | PHILLIPA

Jasmine Atkins is a performer originally from Sydney. She has acted in a variety of university productions, beginning with City University of London's production of *The Fall* (2019) and *Spring Awakening* (2020). Since moving to Canberra in 2021, Jasmine has been involved with theatre at the Australian National University. She played Gonzalo in Shakesoc's *The Tempest* (2021) and Mina in the National University Theatre Society's production of *Dracula* (2022). This is her first production with Canberra Youth Theatre.

CAITLIN BAKER | LIZZIE

Caitlin Baker is an emerging actor, director, and theatre-maker, in her fourth year of Arts/Law (Hon) at ANU. This year Caitlin is a Canberra Youth Theatre Resident Artist, and President of the ANU Shakespeare Society, where she performed in their inaugural production of *Much Ado About Nothing* (2019), and directed *The Tempest* (2021). Caitlin has performed with Canberra Repertory Society in *Grapes of Wrath* (2020), *Brighton Beach Memoirs* (2020), and *The Governor's Family* (2021), *Carpe DM* with Canberra Youth Theatre's Emerge Company (2021), Law Revue's *Paddington 3* (2021) and Alchemy Artistic's *The Boys* (2022). Assistant directing credits for Canberra Youth Theatre include *The Initiation* and *Soul Trading*. Often noted as 'loud' and 'intense', Caitlin is thrilled for you to watch exactly why she should never be allowed near government politics.

MAXINE BEAUMONT | ENSEMBLE

Maxine Beaumont is an actor and singer. Raised with both Filipino and Australian cultures, Maxine is passionate about expressing diverse voices and stories in the Australian arts industry. She is a graduate of ANU, having a Bachelor of Science (Psychology - Honours) and Bachelor of International Security Studies. She also studied music through the ANU School of Music Jazz and Contemporary Music Ensembles and is classically trained in voice. Maxine graduated from Perform Australia with a Certificate IV in Acting for Stage and Screen (2020) and was in the Canberra Youth Theatre Actors Ensemble (2013 - 2014). Her theatre credits include Raquelle in *All That I Am and All That I Have*, the Narrator in *Joseph and the Technicolour Dreamcoat* and Rapunzel in *Into the Woods*. She is delighted to be a current member of Canberra Youth Theatre's 2022 Emerge Company.

NICHOLAS BERMINGHAM | WARREN

Nicholas Bermingham is a mathematics student at the Australian National University who has been involved in theatre since the age of 10. Growing up in Bowral, Nicholas was involved in productions with Magic Box Productions, the Southern Highlands Youth Arts Council, and his high school, Chevalier College. Since moving to Canberra, Nicholas has performed in the National University Theatre Society's production of *Arcadia* (2021) and *Catch 22* (2022) as well as the ANU Shakespeare Society's production of *Twelfth Night* (2021). This is his first production with Canberra Youth Theatre.

ELLA BUCKLEY | MON

Ella Buckley is a passionate performer with a love for the theatre. She has been a part of Canberra's theatre scene for five years, and recently completed her Certificate IV in Acting with Perform Australia. Ella has had the pleasure of performing a variety of shows and characters. Some of her favourite productions include: *Little Girls Alone in The Woods* (2021, Canberra Youth Theatre), *Brighton Beach Memoirs* (2020, Canberra Repertory Society) *Jasper Jones* (2019, Budding Theatre) and *Pride & Prejudice* (2019, Budding Theatre). Currently working as a Workshop Artist with Canberra Youth Theatre, Ella is enthusiastic about advocating for youth theatre. She is delighted to be performing as Mon, and hopes the character will inspire others to identify where a hole is in their life, and to find a way to fill it.

CAST

ASHLEIGH BUTLER | ENSEMBLE

Ashleigh Butler has been training for this role ever since she became a university student in 2019, and proves her dedication to university life by appearing in the UC course guide for 2023. One of her favourite roles on stage was as The Narrator in ChildPlay ACT's *Charlie and the Chocolate Factory,* where she has also directed several shows as part of their school holiday programs. Ashleigh works as a presenter at Questacon, creating explosions (bicarb and vinegar) at the request of small children, and is a member of Canberra Youth Theatre's Emerge Company. Ashleigh is excited to be a part of the *How To Vote* cast and hopes you enjoy the show!

TIM CUSACK | KEV

Tim Cusack began acting at age 14, performing in many plays in high school which only furthered his love for theatre. Tim attended Charles Sturt University in Wagga Wagga where he studied a Bachelor of Stage and Screen (Acting), introducing him to many different approaches of acting and ways to apply himself. Tim has starred in many productions such as *A Midsummer Night's Dream* and *Tales of the Arabian Nights*. After an acting hiatus, he is honoured to be jumping back into it with such an incredible play.

CALLUM DOHERTY | STEW

Callum Doherty is a multi-award losing actor with over ten years' stage experience. Widely considered the Daniel Day-Lewis of Canberra, he rigorously prepared for the role of Stew by sewing his own clothes and maintaining an Australian accent on-and-offstage for the entire rehearsal period. Select credits include *This Changes Everything* (Echo Youth), *Jasper Jones* (Budding Theatre, CAT nomination), *The Full Monty* (SUPA Productions), *Strictly Ballroom* (Canberra Philharmonic Society), *The Addams Family* (The Q, CAT nomination), *The Music Man* (Queanbeyan Players), and *Mary Poppins* (Free Rain Theatre). He is also a Q Young Ambassador and has performed at the Canberra Comedy Festival. This is his first production with Canberra Youth Theatre.

JESSICA GOODING | ENSEMBLE

Jessica Gooding studied drama as a major in college and has been involved with Mockingbird Theatre Company for three years. She completed a two-week residency course at NIDA in 2020, one of the highlights of her acting experience. In April this year, she played the role of Brownyn in Canberra Youth Theatre's *Dags*, her first major production. She is also privileged to be a part of Canberra Youth Theatre's 2022 Emerge Company, and is absolutely thrilled to be part of the exciting premiere of *How To Vote!*

QUINN GOODWIN | ENSEMBLE

Accidental university drop-out Quinn Goodwin has spent her life on the stage, making her debut at the ripe old age of 7 years old. Now with over ten years of experience, she is excited to experience a 'normal' university year in *How to Vote!* Previously working with Canberra Youth Theatre on *Possibility* (2019) and appearing as Meg in *Away* (2020), in 2021 she tried her hand at directing *Legally Blonde the Musical* for University College's annual musical. This year she is a part of Canberra Youth Theatre's Emerge Company. When not on stage she can be found writing numerous film projects and questioning the purpose of an Arts degree.

BLUE HYSLOP | RON

Blue Hyslop has been involved with theatre since 2016. In 2019 they performed in *I Haven't Thought of a Title Yet* for the Sydney Short+Sweet festival, *Machinal* for Narrabundah College, and *The Art of Coarse Acting* and *The Woman in the Window* for Canberra REP. Over the past three years, Blue has performed in four more Canberra REP productions: *The Grapes of Wrath*, *What the Butler Saw*, *Cosi*, and the 2022 production of *Romeo and Juliet*. This year Blue performed in Alchemy Artistic's *The Boys*, and Chaika Theatre's debut work *Three Tall Women*. *How To Vote!* is their second Canberra Youth Theatre show, having worked on the 2021 production of *Two Twenty Somethings*. They are so excited to be working with Canberra Youth Theatre again on such a fascinating piece.

CAST

THEA JADE | ELISE

Thea Jade is thrilled to make her stage debut playing Elise. With a strong screen acting portfolio, she has received over fifteen performance awards and nominations over the last year — most recently 'Most Memorable Performance' by ArtsACT at the 2022 Enlighten film festival. Thea is a 2022 ambassador for Polished Man, a national campaign dedicated to ending violence against women and children. She is devoted to youth advocacy and engagement, and is a part of the core staff at Canberra Youth Theatre, as well as a workshop artist and a member of the Emerge Company: Canberra Youth Theatre's 18-25 year old professional development program.

BREANNA KELLY | ENSEMBLE

Breanna Kelly is excited to be back working with Canberra Youth Theatre after performing as Monica in *Dags* earlier in the year. Breanna is a passionate young actor who has been in the Canberra theatre scene for eight years now. She has performed many roles including Jo March in *Little Women*, Featured Dancer in *Be More Chill* (Budding Theatre), and she directed and performed as Linda in *Blood Brothers* (St Francis Xavier College). In 2021 she played the lead role of Emma in Hawker College's original radio musical *Multiverse Superstar*. She is thrilled to be apart of this exciting new piece of theatre and hopes you enjoy the show.

CLAIRE IMLACH | PRATCHETT

This is Claire Imlach's second year as a part of Canberra Youth Theatre, and she is very excited to be a part of *How To Vote!* Claire grew up in Launceston, Tasmania, where she trained in singing, dancing, and acting from a young age. Her previous credits include *Tarzan*, *Peter Pan* and *The Addams Family*. She now lives in Canberra, where she studies Education at ACU. Claire was a member of Canberra Youth Theatre's Emerge Company in 2021, performing in *Carpe DM*. Claire is excited to be realising the role of Pratchett at the Canberra Theatre Centre.

YVETTE MPINGA | ENSEMBLE

Yvette Mpinga is an eighteen year-old illustrator, writer and animator, originally from South Africa, but now residing in Canberra. She is an autodidact artist, aspiring to be a comedic writer and voice actor. She is currently working on a few animated personal projects, due to be released in late 2022. Yvette has been a part of her high school musical productions, such as *Back to the 80's* and *Beauty and the Beast*, and has played bass guitar in her high school and college jazz bands. This is her first production with Canberra Youth Theatre.

TRACY NOBLE | VICE CHANCELLOR

Tracy Noble is thrilled to be making her Canberra Youth Theatre debut. This year she has performed in Echo Theatre's *Ruthless* at The Q, *The Last Five Years* in Belconnen, and Canberra REP's *Romeo & Juliet*. Other Canberra productions include *Mamma Mia!*, *Shrek* (Free Rain Theatre), *Absurd Person Singular* (Canberra REP), *Assassins* (Everyman Theatre), *Pride and Prejudice* (Budding Theatre), and *Strictly Ballroom* (Philo). With a passion for Broadway musicals, Tracy has performed leading roles in over 20 shows including *The Witches of Eastwick*, *The Little Mermaid*, *Chess*, *Oklahoma*, *Joseph and the Amazing Technicolor Dreamcoat*, *Jesus Christ Superstar*, *A Little Night Music*, and *Passion*. Other professional credits include *South Pacific*, *Phantom*, *Singin' in the Rain*, *Carousel*, *Oliver*, and *A Chorus Line*. Tracy is very grateful for the opportunity to be a part of this new work.

BEN O'LOUGHLIN | ENSEMBLE

Only recently getting into the theatre scene, Ben O'Loughlin has already participated in a number of shows, both on and off stage. On top of studying live theatre production at CIT, Ben is looking forward to also performing in more shows in the years to come.

CAST

JOANNA RICHARDS | TASH

Joanna Richards trained at American Repertory Theatre at Harvard with Moscow Art Theatre Conservatory, performing in *Three Sisters* and *Uncle Vanya*. Stage credits in Canberra include *Twenty Minutes With The Devil*, *Venus in Fur*, *Boys Will Be Boys*, *Widowbird* (Street Theatre), *Belfast Girls* (Echo Theatre), *Much Ado About Nothing* (Lakespeare), and various musicals including *Blood Brothers* and *Fame*. Screen credits include *Rake* and *Whirld*. Joanna is also a screenwriter and playwright, the inaugural recipient of Canberra Youth Theatre's Emerging Playwright Commission, and participated in The Street Theatre's Early Phase and WIFT's Mentor Her programs, and a mentorship with Chips & Gravy Films. Joanna is the first PhD candidate to be accepted into Virginia Haussenger's 50/50 by 2030 Foundation.

MISCHA RIPPON | ANDY

Mischa Rippon has had a short but bountiful acting history, making his debut onto the stage in early 2021 as Septimus Hodge in the National University Theatre Society's production of *Arcadia*. Later that year he appeared as Chaplain Tappman in a stage adaptation of Joseph Heller's famous novel *Catch-22*. This year, he has performed in two separate productions of *Romeo & Juliet*, one with the ANU Shakespeare Society, in which he played Tybalt, and then he changed sides for Canberra REP, as Benvolio. When he's not on stage, Mischa's hobbies include watching *The Simpsons*, quoting *The Simpsons*, and wearing corduroy.

CAMERON ROSE | ENSEMBLE

Cameron Rose is excited and proud to say *How to Vote!* will be her first official theatre production. She has had a blast being a part of the ensemble and the Canberra Youth Theatre has welcomed her into their community with open arms. As well as *How To Vote!* she is a part of the Canberra Youth Theatre Emerge program for 2022. She is really excited to be a part of this production alongside a great cast of other emerging artists.

MARTHA RUSSELL | GERT

Martha Russell is a Sydney-based actress and theatremaker. In 2020 she studied at the Western Australian Academy of Performing Arts, where she received her Diploma of Acting. In 2021 she worked closely with Canberra Youth Theatre as an emerging artist and workshops teacher for primary aged young artists. Her credits with Canberra Youth Theatre include Olive in *Carpe DM*, and Girlfriend in *Two Twenty Somethings Decide to Never Be Stressed About Anything Ever Again. Ever*. Since moving to Sydney in 2022 she has begun working with the Australian Theatre for Young People, as well as pursuing acting and writing across Sydney's independent theatre scene.

JACK SHANAHAN | FIGARO

Jack Shanahan has been an overeager acting enthusiast from a young age. At Canberra Youth Theatre, he was part of the 2021 Emerge Company, which devised an original short play titled *Carpe DM*. In 2022, he appeared in Canberra Repertory Society's productions of *Rosencrantz and Guildenstern Are Dead*, and *Arsenic and Old Lace*. At ANU, Jack performed in numerous productions by the National University Theatre Society and the ANU Shakespeare Society. These included *The Tempest* (NUTS, 2016), *The Island of Dr. Moreau* (NUTS, 2017), *The Physicists* (NUTS, 2018), *Wit* (NUTS, 2018), *Much Ado About Nothing* (ShakeSoc, 2019), and *Macbeth* (ShakeSoc, 2020). Jack has also participated in various comedy revues, and as an improvisor performed at the Sydney Comedy Festival in 2014.

EMILY SMITH | ENSEMBLE

Emily Smith began performing at age 6 in her school's production of *Beauty and The Beast,* and has since become immersed in theatre. Her credits include *Peter Pan*, *The Wizard of Oz* (Brindabella Christian College), *Popstars*, *Away* (Gungahlin College), *Legally Blonde Jr*, *Grease: The Arena Experience*, and *YOUNGHARTS Live* (Harvest Rain), working alongside Thomas Lacey, Christine Anu, Silvie Paladino, and Rhonda Burchmore. Emily worked on Netflix's *Heartbreak High*, Foxtel's *The Twelve,* and was part of the 2022 Quantum Leap project, *Terra Firma*. Emily is a member of Canberra Youth Theatre's Emerge Company. As an autistic performer, Emily hopes to use performance to break down established beliefs and encourage others to be more accepting and embrace what is different.

CAST

THOMAS WARBURTON | ENSEMBLE

Tommy Warburton is an up and coming young actor who has worked with Budding Entertainment and Green Oak Theatre in the past. Tommy is recently new to the theatre scene however, choosing to focus on education before diving head first into acting full time. Even in an ensemble role, Tommy strives himself in taking as much hands on experience as he can get to refine and enhance his over all skill.

SAAR WESTON | ENSEMBLE

Saar Weston is a young actor new to the Canberra scene. He is a Certificate IV Acting graduate from Perform Australia, and undergraduate musical theatre certificate graduate from CQUniversity, as well as various appearances on screen and stage. Saar is also an experienced flautist of 8 years.

MATT WHITE | GILES

Matt White is in his second year at ANU, studying a Bachelor of Science (Psychology) as he ventures out into the wide world of Canberra Theatre. Debuting as Van Helsing in the National University Theatre Society's *Dracula* (2022), he was then coerced by Queanbeyan's Caitlin Baker (Lizzie Somers) into auditioning for Canberra Youth Theatre's 50th anniversary production *How to Vote!*, after she told him "Hey there is this one character who is basically a young liberal who I think you would be perfect for!". Whilst figuring out exactly what she meant by this, he auditioned, which led him to this moment now. He is thrilled to be a part of this stellar production, and hopes you enjoy the show. He also promises that he is, in fact, a nice person despite what Giles and Warren get up to in the play.

CANBERRA YOUTH THEATRE

STAFF

ARTISTIC DIRECTOR & CEO
LUKE ROGERS

ADMINISTRATOR & WORKSHOPS MANAGER
HELEN WOJTAS

ASSOCIATE PRODUCER
BONNIE CURTIS

FINANCE & STRATEGY MANAGER
LOUISE DAVIDSON

MARKETING & ENGAGEMENT MANAGER
CHRISTOPHER CARROLL

ADMINISTRATION & MARKETING COORDINATOR
THEA JADE

RESIDENT ARTISTS
CAITLIN BAKER
SOPHIE TALLIS

COMMISSIONED WRITERS
JOANNA RICHARDS

BOARD
KAREN VICKERY (CHAIR)
CHRIS WAGNER (DEPUTY CHAIR)
PETER HOOLIHAN (SECRETARY)
TESSA HAMMOND (TREASURER)
ELLEN HARVEY
CASSANDRA HOOLIHAN
ADRIANA LAW
CELIA RIDEAUX

WORKSHOP ARTISTS
CAITLIN BAKER
ELLA BUCKLEY
CHRISTOPHER CARROLL
ELLIOT CLEAVES
THEA JADE
ANNA JOHNSTONE
TOBI ODUSOTE
CATHY PETOCZ
RACHEL ROBERTSON

GORMAN ARTS CENTRE
BATMAN STREET BRADDON ACT 2612
02 6248 5057
INFO@CANBERRAYOUTHTHEATRE.COM.AU

CANBERRAYOUTHTHEATRE.COM.AU

  @canberrayouththeatre

www.currency.com.au

Visit Currency Press' website now to:

- Order books
- Browse through our full list of titles including plays, screenplays, theory and reference/criticism, performance handbooks, educational texts and more
- Choose a play for your school or performance group by cast specs
- Seek performance rights
- Find out about performing arts news and sign up for our newsletter
- For students: read our study guides
- For teachers: access free curriculum information and teacher notes

We are also on Facebook and Instagram (@currencypress). Join the conversation!

The performing arts publisher

www.ingramcontent.com/pod-product-compliance
Lightning Source LLC
Chambersburg PA
CBHW050016090426
42734CB00021B/3296